# Learn German with Starter Stories:
# Moni the Goat Boy

HypLern Interlinear Project
www.hyplern.com

First edition: 2025, August

Author: Johanna Spyri
Translation: Kees van den End
Foreword: Camilo Andrés Bonilla Carvajal PhD

ISBN: 978-1-989643-37-2

kees@hyplern.com
www.hyplern.com

# Learn German with Starter Stories: Moni the Goat Boy

*Interlinear German to English*

## Author
Johanna Spyri

## Translation
Kees van den End

HypLern Interlinear Project
www.hyplern.com

# The HypLern Method

Learning a foreign language should not mean leafing through page after page in a bilingual dictionary until one's fingertips begin to hurt. Quite the contrary, through everyday language use, friendly reading, and direct exposure to the language we can get well on our way towards mastery of the vocabulary and grammar needed to read native texts. In this manner, learners can be successful in the foreign language without too much study of grammar paradigms or rules. Indeed, Seneca expresses in his sixth epistle that "Longum iter est per praecepta, breve et efficax per exempla[1]."

The HypLern series constitutes an effort to provide a highly effective tool for experiential foreign language learning. Those who are genuinely interested in utilizing original literary works to learn a foreign language do not have to use conventional graded texts or adapted versions for novice readers. The former only distort the actual essence of literary works, while the latter are highly reduced in vocabulary and relevant content. This collection aims to bring the lively experience of reading stories as directly told by their very authors to foreign language learners.

Most excited adult language learners will at some point seek their teachers' guidance on the process of learning to read in the foreign language rather than seeking out external opinions. However, both teachers and learners lack a general reading technique or strategy. Oftentimes, students undertake the reading task equipped with nothing more than a bilingual dictionary, a grammar book, and lots of courage. These efforts often end in frustration as the student builds mis-constructed nonsensical sentences after many hours spent on an aimless translation drill.

Consequently, we have decided to develop this series of interlinear translations intended to afford a comprehensive edition of unabridged texts. These texts are presented as they were originally written with no changes in word choice or order. As a result, we have a translated piece conveying the true meaning under every word from the original work. Our readers receive then two books in just one volume: the original version and its translation.

The reading task is no longer a laborious exercise of patiently decoding unclear and seemingly complex paragraphs. What's more, reading becomes an enjoyable and meaningful process of cultural, philosophical and linguistic learning. Independent learners can then acquire expressions and vocabulary while understanding pragmatic and socio-cultural dimensions of the target language by reading in it rather than reading about it.

Our proposal, however, does not claim to be a novelty. Interlinear translation is as old as the Spanish tongue, e.g. "glosses of [Saint] Emilianus", interlinear bibles in Old German, and of course James Hamilton's work in the 1800s. About the latter, we remind the readers, that as a revolutionary freethinker he promoted the publication of Greco-Roman classic works and further pieces in diverse languages. His effort, such as ours, sought to lighten the exhausting task of looking words up in large glossaries as an educational practice: "if there is any thing which fills reflecting men with melancholy and regret, it is the waste of mortal time, parental money, and puerile happiness, in the present method of pursuing Latin and Greek[2]".

Additionally, another influential figure in the same line of thought as Hamilton was John Locke. Locke was also the philosopher and translator of the Fabulae AEsopi in an interlinear plan. In 1600, he was already suggesting that interlinear texts, everyday communication, and use of the target language could be the most appropriate ways to achieve language learning:

> ...the true and genuine Way, and that which I would propose, not only as the easiest and best, wherein a Child might, without pains or Chiding, get a Language which others are wont to be whipt for at School six or seven Years together...[3]

---

1   "The journey is long through precepts, but brief and effective through examples". Seneca, Lucius Annaeus. (1961) Ad Lucilium Epistulae Morales, vol. I. London: W. Heinemann.

2   In: Hamilton, James (1829?) History, principles, practice and results of the Hamiltonian system, with answers to the Edinburgh and Westminster reviews; A lecture delivered at Liverpool; and instructions for the use of the books published on the system. Londres: W. Aylott and Co., 8, Pater Noster Row. p. 29.

3   In: Locke, John. (1693) Some thoughts concerning education. Londres: A. and J. Churchill. pp. 196-7.

# Who can benefit from this edition?

We identify three kinds of readers, namely, those who take this work as a search tool, those who want to learn a language by reading authentic materials, and those attempting to read writers in their original language. The HypLern collection constitutes a very effective instrument for all of them.

1. For the first target audience, this edition represents a search tool to connect their mother tongue with that of the writer's. Therefore, they have the opportunity to read over an original literary work in an enriching and certain manner.

2. For the second group, reading every word or idiomatic expression in its actual context of use will yield a strong association between the form, the collocation, and the context. This will have a direct impact on long term learning of passive vocabulary, gradually building genuine reading ability in the original language. This book is an ideal companion not only to independent learners but also to those who take lessons with a teacher. At the same time, the continuous feeling of achievement produced during the process of reading original authors both stimulates and empowers the learner to study[1].

3. Finally, the third kind of reader will notice the same benefits as the previous ones. The proximity of a word and its translation in our interlinear texts is a step further from other collections, such as the Loeb Classical Library. Although their works might be considered the most famous in this genre, the presentation of texts on opposite pages hinders the immediate link between words and their semantic equivalence in our native tongue (or one we have a strong mastery of).

---

1  Some further ways of using the present work include:

1. As you progress through the stories, focus less on the lower line (the English translation). Instead, try to read through the upper line, staying in the foreign language as long as possible.

2. Even if you find glosses or explanatory footnotes about the mechanics of the language, you should make your own hypotheses on word formation and syntactical functions in a sentence. Feel confident about inferring your own language rules and test them progressively. You can also take notes concerning those idiomatic expressions or special language usage that calls your attention for later study.

3. As soon as you finish each text, check the reading in the original version (with no interlinear or parallel translation). This will fulfil the main goal of this

collection: bridging the gap between readers and original literary works, training them to read directly and independently.

# Why interlinear?

Conventionally speaking, tiresome reading in tricky and exhausting circumstances has been the common definition of learning by texts. This collection offers a friendly reading format where the language is not a stumbling block anymore. Contrastively, our collection presents a language as a vehicle through which readers can attain and understand their authors' written ideas.

While learning to read, most people are urged to use the dictionary and distinguish words from multiple entries. We help readers skip this step by providing the proper translation based on the surrounding context. In so doing, readers have the chance to invest energy and time in understanding the text and learning vocabulary; they read quickly and easily like a skilled horseman cantering through a book.

Thereby we stress the fact that our proposal is not new at all. Others have tried the same before, coming up with evident and substantial outcomes. Certainly, we are not pioneers in designing interlinear texts. Nonetheless, we are nowadays the only, and doubtless, the best, in providing you with interlinear foreign language texts.

# Handling instructions

Using this book is very easy. Each text should be read at least three times in order to explore the whole potential of the method. The first phase is devoted to comparing words in the foreign language to those in the mother tongue. This is to say, the upper line is contrasted to the lower line as the following example shows:

| "Ja | natürlich", | war | die | Antwort. |
|-----|-------------|-----|-----|----------|
| Yes | naturally   | was | the | answer   |
|     | of course   |     |     |          |

The second phase of reading focuses on capturing the meaning and sense of the original text. As readers gain practice with the method, they should be able to focus on the target language without getting distracted by the translation. New users of the method, however, may find it helpful to cover the translated lines with a piece of paper as illustrated in the image below. Subsequently, they try to understand the meaning of every word, phrase, and entire sentences in the target language itself, drawing on the translation only when necessary. In this phase, the reader should resist the temptation to look at the translation for every word. In doing so, they will find that they are able to understand a good portion of the text by reading directly in the target language, without the crutch of the translation. This is the skill we are looking to train: the ability to read and understand native materials and enjoy them as native speakers do, that being, directly in the original language.

"Ja natürlich", war die Antwort.
Yes    naturally
       of course

In the final phase, readers will be able to understand the meaning of the text when reading it without additional help. There may be some less common words and phrases which have not cemented themselves yet in the reader's brain, but the majority of the story should not pose any problems. If desired, the reader can use an SRS or some other memorization method to learning these straggling words.

"Ja natürlich", war die Antwort.

Above all, readers will not have to look every word up in a dictionary to read a text in the foreign language. This otherwise wasted time will be spent concentrating on their principal interest. These new readers will tackle authentic texts while learning their vocabulary and expressions to use in further communicative (written or oral) situations. This book is just one work from an overall series with the same purpose. It really helps those who are afraid of having "poor vocabulary" to feel confident about reading directly in the language. To all of them and to all of you, welcome to the amazing experience of living a foreign language!

## Additional tools

Check out shop.hyplern.com or contact us at info@hyplern.com for free mp3s (if available) and free empty (untranslated) versions of the eBooks that we have on offer.

For some of the older eBooks and paperbacks we have Windows, iOS and Android apps available that, next to the interlinear format, allow for a pop-up format, where hovering over a word or clicking on it gives you its meaning. The apps also have any mp3s, if available, and integrated vocabulary practice.

Visit the site hyplern.com for the same functionality online. This is where we will be working non-stop to make all our material available in multiple formats, including audio where available, and vocabulary practice.

# Table of Contents

| Chapter | Page |
|---|---|

# Der Moni fühlt sich wohl
## *Moni Feels Himself Well*

Um zu dem Badehaus Fideris zu gelangen, muß
In order to the bathhouse Fideris to reach must
hotel of

man steil und lang die Höhe hinaufsteigen,
one steep and long the height climb up
altitude

nachdem man die Straße verlassen hat, die sich
after one the road leave has which itself
left

durch das lange Tal des Prättigau nach oben
through the long valley of Prättigau to up
upwards

schlängelt. So mühsam keuchen dann die Pferde
meanders So tediously gasp then the horses

den Berg hinauf, daß man lieber aussteigt und
the mountain up (so)that one rather gets out and

zu Fuß die grüne Höhe erreicht.
to foot the green height reaches
on

Nach einem längeren Anstieg kommt man erst
After a longer rise comes one first

zum — Dorf — Fideris, — das — auf — der — freundlichen,
to the — village — Fideris — that — upon — the — friendly

grünen — Anhöhe — liegt. — Von — da — geht — es — weiter — in
green — elevation — lies — From — there — goes — it — further — to

die — Berge — hinein, — bis — das — einsame — Gebäude — des
the — mountains — into — until — the — lonely — buildings — of the

Badeortes — auftaucht, — überall — von — felsigen — Höhen
bathing-place / resort — pop up — everywhere — from / by — rocky — heights

umgeben. — Dort — oben — wachsen — nur — noch — Tannen,
surrounded — There — above — grow — only — still — fir trees

die — die — Höhen — und — Felsen — ringsum — bedecken. — Es
which — the — heights — and — rocks — all around — cover — It

sähe — alles — ziemlich — düster — aus, — wenn — nicht
would look (aussehen; look) — all — rather — bleak — -out- — when — not

überall — aus — dem — niederen — Weidegras — die — schönen
everywhere — from — the — lower — pasture grass — the — beautiful

Bergblümchen — mit — ihren — glänzenden — Farben
mountain flowers — with — their — shining — colors

**hervorguckten.**
peep out

**An einem hellen Sommerabend traten zwei Damen**
On one clear summer evening stepped two ladies

**aus dem Badehaus und gingen auf dem schmalen**
out of the Bathhouse and went up the narrow
Hotel

**Fußweg dahin, der unweit des Hauses beginnt**
footpath there to which not far of the house begins
from the

**und bald sehr steil bis zu den hoch**
and (is) soon very steep until to the high

**anfragenden Felsen hinaufsteigt. An dem ersten**
demanding rocks climbs up at that first
steep

**Vorsprung blieben sie stehen und schauten um**
ledge remained they stand and looked around

**sich, denn sie waren eben erst in dem Bad**
themselves then they were just only to the bath
since had hotel

**angekommen.**
arrived

"Lustig ist's nicht hier oben, Tante", sagte jetzt die
Funny is it not here above Aunt said now the

Jüngere, indem sie die Landschaft betrachtete.
younger while they the landscape considered

"Lauter Felsen und Tannenwälder und dann wieder
only rocks and fir forests and then again

ein Berg und noch einmal Tannen darauf.
a mountain and yet once more fir trees there after

Wenn wir sechs Wochen hier bleiben sollen, dann
when we six weeks here stay must then

wollte ich, es wäre hier und da auch noch
wanted I it were here and there also more

etwas Lustigeres zu sehen."
something amusing to see

"Lustig wird's jedenfalls nicht sein, wenn du hier
Funny it will in any case not be when you here

oben dein Brillantenkreuz verlierst, Paula",
above your diamond cross lose Paula

5

entgegnete die Tante, während sie das rote
replied the aunt while she the red

Samtband zusammenknüpfte, an dem das
velvet ribbon knotted together on which that

funkelnde Kreuz hing. "Es ist das drittemal, daß
sparkling cross hung it is the third time that

ich das Band festmache, seit wir angekommen
I the ribbon secure since we arrived

sind. Ich weiß nicht, wo es fehlt, ob an dir
are I know not where it lacks whether on you
have where is the fault

oder an dem Band, aber das weiß ich, daß du
or on the ribbon but it know I that you

jammern wirst, wenn es verloren ist."
crying will be when it lost is

"Nein, nein", rief Paula lebhaft aus, "das Kreuz
No no called Paula lively out the cross
(ausrufen; exclaim)

darf nicht verlorengehen, um keinen Preis, es ist
may not get lost at no cost it is
must any

noch von der Großmutter und ist mein größter
still from the grandmother and is my greatest

Schatz!"
treasure

Paula ergriff selbst noch das Band und machte
Paula gripped even still the ribbon and made

zwei, drei Knoten hinein, damit es festhalte.
two three knots inside there-with it held fast

Plötzlich spitzte sie die Ohren. "Hör, hör, Tante,
suddenly pointed she the ears Hear hear Aunt

jetzt kommt aber wirklich etwas Lustiges."
now comes however truly something amusing

Hoch oben erscholl ein fröhlicher Gesang.
High above sounded a happy singing

Zwischendurch kam ein langer, schallender Jodler,
Occasionally came a long resounding yodel

dann wurde wieder gesungen. Die Damen schauten
then was again sung The ladies looked

aufwärts, konnten aber nichts Lebendiges
upwards (they) could however nothing living

entdecken. Der Fußweg ging in großen
discover The footpath went in great

Serpentinen, oft zwischen hohem Gebüsch und
serpentines often between high bushes and

wieder zwischen vorstehenden Bergabhängen durch,
back between protruding mountain slopes through

so daß man von unten immer nur kurze
so that one from below always just short

Stückchen davon erblicken konnte. Aber jetzt
pieces of it glimpse could however now

wurde es plötzlich lebendig auf dem Pfad, oben
was it suddenly lively on the path above

und unten, auf allen Stellen, wo der schmale
and below on all places where the narrow

Weg gesehen werden konnte, und immer lauter
path seen become could and ever louder

und näher tönte der Gesang.
and closer sounded the singing

"Sieh, sieh, Tante, dort! Hier! Sieh da! Sieh da!"
See see Aunt there Here See there See there

rief Paula mit großem Vergnügen. Und ehe
exclaimed Paula with great pleasure And before

die Tante sich's versah, kamen drei, vier Geißen
the Aunt herself it managed came three four goats

in Sprüngen daher und immer mehr, immer
in jumps therefore and always more always

mehr, und jede hatte ein Glöcklein am Hals. Die
more and each had a little bell on the neck These

läuteten von allen Seiten her, und mitten in
rang from all sides away and (in the) middle in

einem Rudel kam der Geißbub herabgesprungen
a pack came the goat boy jumped down

und sang eben noch sein Lied zu Ende:
and sang just still his song to (the) end

"Und   im   Winter  bleib  ich  fröhlich,
And  in the  winter  remain  I    happy

Weil's    Weinen  nichts  nützt,
Because it  crying    not   is useful

Und  weil  ihm  sowieso  der  Frühling
And  since  him   anyway   the    spring

Auf  den  Fersen  schon  sitzt."
at   the   heels   already  sits

Dann  ließ  er  einen  ungeheuren  Jodel  erschallen.
Then   let  he   a    tremendous    yodel    resound

Und  auf  einmal  stand  er  mit  seinem  Rudel  dicht
And   at   once   stood  he  with   his     pack   close

vor  den  Damen,  denn  mit  seinen  nackten  Füßen
before  the  ladies   then  with   his      bare    feet

sprang  er  genauso  flink  und  leise  wie  seine
leapt   he  just as  nimble  and  softly  as   his

Tierchen.
little animals

"Guten Abend wünsche ich", sagte er, indem er die
Good evening wish I said he while he the

beiden lustig anschaute, und wollte weiterziehen.
both merrily looked at and would move on

Aber der Geißbub mit den fröhlichen Augen
However the goat boy with the joyful eyes

gefiel den Damen. "Wart ein wenig", sagte Paula,
pleased the ladies Wait a little said Paula
minute

"bist du der Geißbub von Fideris? Hast du Geißen
are you the goat boy of Fideris Have you goats

aus dem Dorf unten?"
from the village below

"Ja natürlich", war die Antwort.
Yes naturally was the answer
of course

"Gehst du alle Tage mit ihnen da hinauf?"
Go you all days with them there up

"Ja freilich."
Yes freely
of course

"So, so, und wie heißt du denn?"
So   so   and   how   called   you   then

"Moni   heiße   ich."
Moni   call (myself)   I

"Willst   du   mir   auch   das   Lied   einmal   singen,   das
Will   you   me   also   the   song   once more   sing   that

du   eben   gesungen   hast?
you   just   sung   have

Wir   haben   erst   einen   Vers   gehört."
We   have   only   one   verse   heard

"Das   ist   zu   lang", erklärte   Moni, "es   wird   zu   spät
It   is   too   long   explained   Moni   it   becomes   too   late

für   die   Geißen,   sie   müssen   heim."   Er   rückte   sein
for   the   goats   they   must (go)   home   He   pulled   his

altes   Hütchen   zurecht,   schwang   seine   Rute   in   der
old   little hat   right   swung   his   rod   in   the
straight

Luft   und   rief   den   Geißen   zu,   die   schon
air   and   called   the   goats   to (himself)   who   already

überall zu nagen angefangen hatten: "Heim!
everywhere to gnaw started had Home

Heim!"
Home

"So singst du mir's doch ein andermal, Moni, nicht
So sing you me yet an other time Moni not

wahr?" rief ihm
true called him

Paula nach.
Paula after

"Ja, das will ich und gute Nacht!" rief er zurück,
Yes that will I and good night called he back

setzte sich nun mit den Geißen in Trab, und in
put himself now with the goats in trot and in

kurzer Zeit stand die ganze Herde unten, wenige
short time stood the whole herd below a few

Schritte vom Badehaus bei dem Hintergebäude
steps from the Bathhouse by the back building

13

still. Denn hier hatte Moni die Geißen, die zum
quiet Then here had Moni the goats which to the

Haus gehörten, die schöne weiße und die
house belonged the beautiful white and the

schwarze mit dem zierlichen Zicklein abzugeben.
black (ones) with the dainty kid (goat) to deliver

Moni behandelte letzteres mit größter Sorgfalt,
Moni treated the latter with greatest care

denn es war ein zartes Tierchen, und er liebte es
because it was a tender little animal and he loved it

von allen am meisten. Es war auch so
from all -at- the most It was also so

anhänglich, daß es ihm den ganzen Tag immer
affectionate that it him the whole day always

nachlief. Er zog es auch jetzt ganz zärtlich zu
ran after He pulled it also now completely tender to

sich und stellte es in seinen Stall hinein. Dann
himself and set it in his stable inside Then

sagte er: "So, Mäggerli, nun schlaf gut, du bist
said he So Mäggerli now sleep well you are

müde. Es ist sehr weit bis dort hinauf, und du
tired It is very far until there up and you

bist noch so klein. Leg dich jetzt nur gleich
are still so small Lay you now only immediately

hin, siehst du, so in das gute Stroh hinein."
away see you so in the good straw inside
down like that

Nachdem er so das Mäggerli zur Ruhe gebettet
After he so the Mäggerli to the rest bedded

hatte, zog er eilig weiter mit seiner Schar, erst
had pulled he hurriedly further with his flock first
moved

vor dem Badehaus den Hügel hinauf und dann
before the bathhouse the hill up and then

die Straße hinunter dem Dorf zu. Hier nahm er
the street down the village to Here took he

sein Hörnchen vor den Mund und blies so
his little horn before the mouth and blew so

gewaltig hinein, daß es dröhnte bis weit ins Tal
violently inside that it boomed until far in the valley

hinab. Von allen verstreuten Höfen her kamen
down From all scattered courtyards away came

jetzt die Kinder gelaufen, jedes stürzte auf seine
now the children run each rushed on its

Geiß, die es aus der Ferne schon kannte. Und
goat which it from the distance already knew And

von den nahen Häusern her kam hier eine Frau
from the close houses away came here a woman

und dort eine, faßte ihr Geißlein am Strick oder
and there one seized her kid (goat) at the rope or

am Horn, und in kurzer Zeit war die ganze
at the horn and in short time was the whole

Herde auseinandergestoben, und jedes Tierlein
herd out-each-other-rushed and each little animal
separated

kam an seinen Ort. Zuletzt stand der Moni noch
came at its place At last stood the Moni still

allein mit der Braunen, seiner eigenen Geiß, und
alone with the brown (one) his own goat and

mit ihr ging er zu dem Häuschen am
with her went he to the little house at the

Bergabhang, wo schon die Großmutter ihn in der
downhill slope where already the grandmother him in the

Tür erwartete.
door expected

"Ist alles gut gegangen, Moni?" fragte sie
Is everything good went Moni asked she
    Did everything go well

freundlich, führte dann die Braune in den Stall
friendly led then the brown (one) in the stable

und fing gleich an, sie zu melken. Die
and caught immediately on her to milk The
    started immediately

Großmutter war noch eine rüstige Frau und
grandmother was still a sprightly woman and

besorgte alles selbst im Haus und im Stall
cared for everything herself in the house and in the stable

und hielt überall Ordnung. Moni stand in der
and held everywhere order Moni stood in the

Stalltür und schaute der Großmutter zu. Als das
stable door and looked the grandmother at As the

Melken beendet war, trat sie ins Häuschen und
milking finished was stepped she in the little house and

sagte: "Komm, Moni, du wirst Hunger haben."
said Come Moni you will hunger have
hungry be

Sie hatte auch schon alles hergerichtet. Moni
She had also already everything prepared Moni

konnte sich sofort an den Tisch setzen. Sie
could himself immediately at the table set She

nahm neben ihm Platz. Obwohl es nur eine
took beside him place Although it only a
sat beside him

Schüssel voll Maisbrei mit der Milch der
dish full (of) corn porridge with the milk the

Braunen gab, so ließ sich's Moni doch herrlich
brown (one) gave so let itself it Moni indeed wonderfully
was

schmecken. Dabei erzählte er der Großmutter,
taste There-by told he the grandmother

was er den Tag über erlebt hatte, und sobald
what he the day over experienced had and as soon as
through

er sein Mahl beendet hatte, zog er sich auf sein
he his meal finished had drew he himself on his

Lager zurück, denn er mußte sich ja früh am
bed back then he must himself yes early at the

Morgen wieder mit der Herde auf den Weg
morning again with the herd on the way

machen.
make

Auf diese Weise hatte Moni schon zwei Sommer
On this manner had Moni already two summers

verbracht, so lange schon war er Geißbub. Er war
spent so long already was he goat boy He was

jetzt so an dieses Leben gewöhnt und mit seinen
now so on this life used and with his

Tierchen verbunden, daß er sich's gar nicht
little animal connected that he himself it at all not

anders denken konnte. Mit seiner Großmutter
different think could With his grandmother

lebte Moni zusammen, solange er sich besinnen
lived Moni together as long (as) he himself reflect

konnte. Seine Mutter war gestorben, als er noch
could His mother was died as he still
had

ganz klein war. Sein Vater zog bald danach
completely small was His father pulled soon afterwards
moved

mit anderen zum Kriegsdienst nach Neapel, um
with others to the military service to Naples for

etwas zu verdienen, denn er meinte, das gehe
something to earn then he thought that go

dort schneller.
there faster

Die Mutter seiner Frau war auch arm, aber sie
The mother of his wife was also poor but she

nahm auf der Stelle das verlassene Büblein ihrer
took on the spot the abandoned little boy of her

Tochter, den kleinen Salomon, zu sich und teilte
daughter the small Solomon to herself and shared

mit ihm, was sie hatte. Es lag auch ein Segen
with him what she had It lay also a blessing
There

auf ihrem Häuschen, und noch nie hatte sie Not
on her little house and still never had she need

leiden müssen.
suffer must

Die brave, alte Elsbeth war auch im ganzen Dorf
The brave old Elsbeth was also in the whole village

beliebt, und als vor zwei Jahren ein anderer
loved and as before two years an other

Geißbub ausgewählt wurde, da fielen alle
goat boy selected became there fell all

Stimmen einstimmig auf den Moni. Denn jeder
voices unanimously on the Moni Since each

gönnte es der arbeitsamen Elsbeth, daß nun Moni
granted it the hard working Elsbeth that now Moni

auch etwas verdienen konnte. Die fromme
also something earn could The pious

Großmutter hatte den Moni keinen Morgen
grandmother had the Moni no morning

weggehen lassen, ohne daß sie ihm sagte: "Moni,
away go let without that she him said Moni

vergiß nicht, wie nah du dort oben dem lieben
forget not how near you there above the dear

Gott bist und daß er alles sieht und hört. Du
god are and that he everything sees and hears You

kannst vor seinen Augen nichts verbergen. Aber
can before his eyes nothing hide But

vergiß auch nicht, daß er in deiner Nähe ist,
forget also not that he in your proximity is

um dir zu helfen. Daher mußt du dich nie
for you to help There-from must you yourself never

fürchten, und wenn du dort oben keine Menschen
fear       and   when  you  there  above    no      people

herbeirufen kannst, rufe du nur zum lieben Gott
summon        can    call you only to the dear    god

in der Not, er hört dich    gleich     und kommt dir
in  the  need  he  hears  you  immediately  and  comes   you

zur   Hilfe."
to the    help

So  zog  Moni von Anfang an voller Zuversicht auf
So  pulled  Moni  from  beginning  on   full   confidence   on
                                                              to

die einsamen Höhen und die höchsten Felsen und
the    lonely    heights  and  the  highest    cliffs   and

hatte  nie  die  leiseste  Furcht  noch  Schrecken,
had   never  the  quietest   fear    nor     fright

denn  er  dachte  immer:  Je  höher  hinauf,  desto
then   he  thought  always  The  higher    up      the

näher bin ich beim lieben Gott und desto sicherer
closer  am  I  to the  dear   god  and  the  more sure

in allem, was mir begegnen kann. So hatte Moni
in all what me meet can So had Moni
of

weder Sorge noch Kummer und konnte sich
neither worry nor sorrow and could himself

freuen an allem, was er erlebte vom Morgen
enjoy on all what he experienced from the morning

bis zum Abend. Und es war kein Wunder, daß er
until to the evening And it was no miracle that he

immer pfiff und sang und jodelte, denn er
always whistled and sang and yodeled then he

mußte seiner großen Fröhlichkeit Luft machen.
must his large happiness air make

# Monis Leben auf dem Berg
## *Moni's Life on the Mountain*

Am folgenden Morgen erwachte Paula so früh wie
At the following morning woke up Paula so early as
next

sonst nie, ein lauter Gesang hatte sie aus dem
otherwise never a loud singing had her from the

Schlaf geweckt. "Da ist gewiß schon der
sleep awakened There is certainly already the

Geißbub", sagte sie, sprang aus dem Bett und lief
goat boy said she jumped from the bed and ran

ans Fenster.
to the window

Richtig, mit frischen, roten Backen stand der Moni
Correct with fresh red cakes stood the Moni

im Hof und hatte eben die alte Geiß und das
in the court and had just the old goat and the

Zicklein aus dem Stall geholt. Jetzt schwang er
kid from the stable fetched Now swung he

seine Rute in der Luft, die Geißen hüpften und
his rod in the air the goats hopped and

sprangen um ihn herum, und nun ging's vorwärts
jumped for him around and now went it further

mit der ganzen Schar. Und plötzlich erhob Moni
with the whole herd And suddenly raised Moni

seine Stimme wieder und sang, daß es von den
his voice again and sang that it from the

Bergen widerhallte:
mountains echoed

"Dort droben in den Tannen
THere up there in the fir trees

Singen die Vögel im Chor,
Sing the birds in the choir

Und hat's eine Weile geregnet,
And had it a while rained

Kommt die Sonne wieder vor."
Comes the sun again before

"Heute muß er mir einmal sein ganzes Lied
Today must he me once his whole song

singen", sagte Paula, denn jetzt war Moni
sing said Paula then now was Moni

verschwunden, und sie konnte seinen fernen
disappeared and she could his distant

Gesang nicht mehr verstehen.
singing not (any)more understand
                              hear

Am Himmel zogen noch die roten Morgenwolken
At the sky pulled still the red morning clouds

dahin, und ein frischer Bergwind rauschte dem
there to and a fresh mountain wind rushed the
away

Moni um die Ohren, als er berganstieg. Das
Moni around the ears as he mountain-up-rose That
                              moved up the mountain

war ihm gerade recht. Vor Wohlbehagen jodelte
was him just right Before pleasure yodeled
                          Of

er vom ersten Bergvorsprung so gewaltig ins
he from the first mountain ledge so enormously in the

Tal hinab, daß mancher Schläfer unten im
valley down that many sleepers under in the

Badehaus erstaunt die Augen aufschlug. Er machte
bathhouse astonished the eyes upstruck He made
hotel opened

sie aber gleich wieder zu, denn er kannte den
them but immediately again to then he knew the

Ton und wußte, daß er nun noch ein Stündchen
tone and knew that he now still a little hour

Schlaf zugeben konnte, denn der Geißbub kam
(to) sleep concede could then the goat boy came

immer so früh. Inzwischen kletterte Moni mit
always so early In the meantime climbed Moni with

seinen Geißen eine Stunde lang weiter und weiter
his goats an hour long further and further

hinauf, bis hoch zu den Felsen.
up until high to the rocks

Immer weiter und immer schöner war es um
Always further and always (more) beautiful was it for

den Moni geworden, je höher er hinaufkam. Von
the Moni become the higher he came up From

Zeit zu Zeit guckte er um sich, dann schaute
time to time looked he around himself then looked

er zu dem hellen Himmel auf, der nun immer
he to the bright sky on which now always

blauer wurde. Dann fing er aus vollem Hals zu
more blue became Then caught he from full neck to
started

singen an, immer lauter und immer fröhlicher, je
sing on always only and always happier the

höher er kam:
higher he came

Dort droben in den Tannen
There up there in the fir trees

Singen die Vögel im Chor,
Sing the birds in the choir

**Und hat's eine Weile geregnet,**
And had it a while rained

**Kommt die Sonne wieder vor.**
Comes the sun again before
in front

**Und die Sonne und die Sterne**
And the sun and the stars

**Und den Mond bei der Nacht,**
And the moon at the night

**Die hat der liebe Gott uns Zur Freude gemacht.**
Which has the love god us to the joy made

**Im Frühling gibt's Blumen,**
In the spring gives it flowers
will there be

**Die sind gelb und sind rot,**
They are yellow and are red

**Und so blau ist der Himmel,**
And so blue is the sky

**Und ich freu mich fast zu Tod.**
and I rejoice myself almost to death

Und im Sommer gibt's Beeren,
And in the summer gives it berries
will there be

Und geht's gut, so gibt's viel,
And goes it well so gives it much
will there be

Und die roten und die schwarzen,
And the red and the black

Eß ich alle vom Stiel.
Eat I all from the stem

Hat's im Hag wieder Nüsse,
had it in the hedge again nuts

So weiß ich wie's tut,
So know I how it does

Wo die Geißen gern nagen,
Where the goats gladly gnaw

Sind die Kräutlein auch gut.
Are the little herbs also good

Und im Winter bin ich fröhlich,
And in the winter am I happy

Weil's     Weinen nichts nützt,
Because it    cry     nothing   is useful to

Und   weil   ihm sowieso der   Frühling,
And   because him   anyway   the     spring

Auf den Fersen schon sitzt.
On   the   heels    already   sits

Jetzt war die Anhöhe erreicht,    wo    er gewöhnlich
Now   was   the   elevation   reached   where   he     usually

   blieb    und    sich    auch heute ausruhen wollte. Das
remained   and   himself   also   today     rest      wanted    It

war eine kleine, grüne Hochebene mit   einem   so
was    a     little    green   height-flat   with    a      so
                               plateau

weiten Vorsprung, daß man von dem freien Punkt
wide    ledge     that one from the   free   point

  ringsumher      und     weiter,   weit     ins      Tal
in a circle around   and    further    far   in the   valley

hinabsehen konnte. Dieser Vorsprung    hieß     die
down see     could   This     ledge     was called   the

Felsenkanzel, und hier konnte Moni oft
rock-pulpit and here could Moni often

stundenlang verweilen und um sich schauen
hours long linger and around himself watch

und vor sich hin pfeifen, während seine
and before himself away whistle while his

Tierlein ganz gemütlich ihre Kräuter suchten.
little animals completely relaxed their herbs searched

Sobald Moni angekommen war, nahm er seinen
As soon as Moni arrived was took he his

kleinen Proviantsack vom Rücken und legte ihn
small food-bag from the back and put it

in eine kleine Höhle des Bodens, die er selbst
in a little hollow of the bottom which he himself
ground

dafür gegraben hatte. Dann trat er auf die
therefore dug had Then stepped he on the

Felsenkanzel hinaus und warf sich auf den Boden,
rock-pulpit out and threw himself on the ground

um sich einmal so recht wohl sein zu lassen.
for himself once so right well be to let

Der Himmel war jetzt dunkelblau geworden.
The sky was now dark blue become

Drüben waren die hohen Berge mit den in den
Over there were the high mountains with the in the

Himmel ragenden Zacken und großen Eisfeldern
sky raging spikes and large ice-fields

zum Vorschein gekommen, und unten leuchtete
to the fore come and under lit

weithin das grüne Tal im Morgenglanz. Moni
widely the green valley in the morning-shine Moni

lag da, schaute umher, sang und pfiff. Der
lay there looked around sang and whistled The

Bergwind kühlte ihm das warme Gesicht, und
mountain-wind refreshed him the warm face and

hörte er einmal zu pfeifen auf, so pfiffen die Vögel
heard he once to whistle up so piped the birds
if he stopped whistling whistled

über ihm noch viel lustiger und flogen in den
over him still much merrier and flew in the

blauen Himmel hinauf. Der Moni fühlte sich
blue sky up The Moni felt himself

unbeschreiblich wohl. Von Zeit zu Zeit kam das
indescribably well From time to time came the

Mäggerli zu ihm und strich ein wenig mit seinem
Mäggerli to him and brushed a little with its

Kopf über Monis Schulter, wie die Geiß es immer
head over Moni's shoulder as the goat it always

tat. Dann meckerte es ganz liebevoll, ging auf
did Then bleated it completely full of love went on

die andere Seite von Moni und strich wieder den
the other side of Moni and brushed again the

Kopf über seine Schulter. Auch von den anderen
head over his shoulder Also from the other

Geißen kam bald diese, bald jene, um nach dem
goats came soon this one soon that one for after the
then then

**Hirten zu sehen, und jede hatte ihre eigene**
shepherd to see and each had her own

**Weise, ihm ihre Zärtlichkeit zu zeigen.**
manner him her tenderness to show

**Die Braune, seine eigene Geiß, kam zu ihm und**
The brown (one) his own goat came to him and

**schaute nach, ob auch alles mit ihm in**
looked after whether also everything with him in

**Ordnung sei. Sie stand dann da und schaute ihn**
order be She stood then there and looked him

**an, bis er sagte: "Ja, ja, Braunli, es ist schon**
at until he said Yes yes little brown one it is already

**recht, geh nur wieder zum Futter." Eine Geiß**
right go only again to the fodder A goat

**hieß die Schwalbe, weil sie so schmal und**
was called the swallow because she so small and

**flink war und überall hineinschoß, wie die**
nimble was and everywhere to-shot as the

Schwalben in ihre Löcher. Sie sprang so ungestüm
swallows in their holes She jumped so impetuously

auf den Moni los, daß sie ihn wohl umgeworfen
on the Moni loose that she him well knocked over

hätte, wäre er nicht schon auf dem Boden
had would be he not already on the ground

gelegen. Gleich darauf lief sie wieder davon.
lied Immediately thereupon ran she again there-from

Die glänzende Schwarze, die Geiß des Wirts im
The shiny black (one) the goat of the owner in the

Badehaus, Mäggerlis Mutter, war ein wenig stolz.
bathhouse Mäggerli's mother was a little proud
hotel

Sie kam nur auf ein paar Schritte Entfernung
She came only on a few steps distance

heran, schaute mit erhobenem Kopf zu dem Moni
near looked with raised head to the Moni

hin, als wollte sie sich nicht zu vertraulich zeigen
away as wanted she herself not too confidentially show

und ging dann wieder ihrer Wege. Der große
and went then again her road The great

Sultan aber, der Bock, zeigte sich immer nur
Sultan however the buck showed himself always only

einmal und drückte dann alle weg, die er in
once and squeezed then everyone away who he in

Monis Nähe traf. Dann meckerte er
Moni's proximity encountered Then bleated he

einigemale so bedeutungsvoll, als habe er
a few times so meaningful as have he

Mitteilungen abzugeben über den Zustand der
information to deliver about the condition of the

Herde, als deren Anführer er sich fühlte.
herd as whose leader he himself felt

Nur das kleine Mäggerli ließ sich niemals von
Only the little Mäggerli let itself never from

seinem Beschützer verdrängen. Wenn der Bock
his defender force away When the buck

kam und wollte es wegdrücken, so kroch es so
came and wanted it force away so crept it so

tief unter Monis Arm oder Kopf, daß der große
deep under Moni's arm or head that the great

Sultan nicht wagte, näher zu kommen. Unter
Sultan not dared closer to come Under

Monis Schutz fürchtete sich das Zicklein auch
Moni's protection feared itself the kid also

kein bißchen mehr vor dem Sultan, vor dem
not (a) bit (any)more before the Sultan, before whom
of

es sonst erzitterte, wenn es in seine Nähe
it otherwise trembled when it in his proximity
would tremble

kam.
came

So war der sonnige Morgen vergangen. Moni hatte
So was the sunny morning gone away Moni had
passed

schon sein Mittagessen verzehrt und stand nun
already his lunch digested and stood now

nachdenklich auf seinen Stecken gestützt, den er
thoughtful on his stick supported which he
leaning

hier oben öfters brauchte. Denn er war ihm beim
here above often needed Then he was him at the
it

Auf- und Abstieg eine große Hilfe. Er dachte
up and down-rise a great help he thought
descend

nach, ob er eine neue Seite der Felsen
after whether he a new side of the rocks

besteigen wollte. Denn an diesem Nachmittag
climb wanted Then on this afternoon

wollte er mit den Geißen höher hinauf, die Frage
wanted he with the goats higher up the question

war nur, nach welcher Seite? Er entschied sich
was only to which side He decided himself

für die linke, denn dort ging es zu den drei
for the left then there went it to the three

Drachensteinen, um die herum so zartes
dragon stones around which around so tender

Buschwerk wuchs, daß es ein wahres Festessen für
bush-work grew that it a true feast-food for
bushes

die Geißen war.
the goats was

Der Weg war steil, und oben waren gefährliche
The way was steep and above were dangerous

Stellen an der schroffen Felswand, aber er wußte
places on the rugged rock-wall but he knew

einen sicheren Weg. Und die Geißen waren ja
a secure way And the goats were yes

vernünftig und verliefen sich nicht so leicht.
smart and went off themselves not so easily
stumbled

Er ging bergauf, und lustig kletterten ihm alle
he went mountain up and merrily climbed him all

seine Geißen nach. Sie waren bald vor, bald
his goats after They were soon before soon
then in front then

hinter ihm, das kleine Mäggerli blieb immer ganz
behind him the little Mäggerli remained always all

in seiner Nähe. Manchmal hielt er es fest und
in his proximity Sometimes held he it firmly and

zog es mit sich, wenn eine steile Stelle kam. Es
pulled it with himself when a steep spot came It

ging aber alles gut, und nun waren sie
went however everything well and now were they

oben, und mit hohen Sprüngen rannten die Geißen
up and with high jumps ran the goats

zu den grünen Büschen hin, denn sie erkannten
to the green shrubs away then they recognized
since

das gute Futter, das sie schon öfter hier oben
the good fodder that she already more often here above

abgenagt hatten.
gnawed off had

"Nur zahm! Nur zahm!" mahnte Moni, "und stoßt
Only tame Only tame warned Moni and bump
gentle gentle

einander nicht an den steilen Stellen, es könnte
each other not on the steep places it could

leicht eines abstürzen und hätte die Beine
easy one crash down and had the legs
would

gebrochen. Schwalbe! Schwalbe! Was kommt denn
broken Swallow Swallow What comes then
break

dir in den Sinn?" rief er jetzt voller Aufregung.
you in the mind called he now full (of) excitement

Denn die flinke Geiß war über die hohen
then the nimble goat was over the high

Drachensteine hinaufgeklettert, stand jetzt auf dem
dragonstones up-climbed stood now on the

äußersten Rand des einen Steins und guckte von
extreme edge of the one stone and looked from

da ganz vorwitzig auf ihn herunter. Er
there completely cheeky on him down He

kletterte eilig hinauf, denn nur noch ein
climbed hurriedly up then only still a

einziger Tritt, und die Schwalbe lag unten im
single step and the swallow lay under in the

Abgrund. Moni war sehr behend, in wenigen
chasm Moni was very swift in few

Minuten hatte er den Stein erklettert und mit
minutes had he the stone climbed and with

einem schnellen Griff die Schwalbe am Bein
a quick grab the swallow at the leg

erfaßt und zurückgezogen. "Komm du jetzt mit
grasped and pulled back Come you now with

mir, du unvernünftiges Tierlein du", schalt Moni
me you senseless little animal you rang out Moni

und zog die Schwalbe mit sich herunter zu den
and pulled the swallow with himself down to the

anderen. Er hielt sie noch ein Weilchen fest, bis
others He held her still a while firmly until

sie nicht mehr ans Fortlaufen dachte.
she not (any)more to the run away thought
thought of running away

"Wo ist das Mäggerli?" schrie Moni plötzlich auf,
Where is the Mäggerli cried Moni suddenly up

der die Schwarze erblickte, wie sie allein an einer
who the black (one) saw as she alone on a

steilen Stelle stand und nichts fraß, sondern ruhig
steep spot stood and nothing ate but calm

umherschaute. Immer war das junge Geißlein
around looked always was the young kid

neben Moni, oder es lief seiner Mutter nach.
besides Moni or it ran its mother after

"Wo hast du dein Zicklein, Schwarze?" rief er
Where have you your kid black (one) called he

erschrocken und sprang auf die Geiß zu. Sie
frightened and jumped on the goat towards She

war ganz sonderbar, fraß nicht, blieb immer
was completely strange ate not remained always

auf demselben Platz stehen und spitzte verdächtig
on the same place stand and pointed suspicious

die Ohren. Moni stellte sich dicht neben sie und
the ears Moni set himself close beside she and

schaute hinauf und hinab. Jetzt hörte er ein leises,
looked up and down Now heard he a slight

jammerndes Meckern. Das war Mäggerlis Stimme,
wailing bleat That was Mäggerli's voice

sie kam von unten herauf, so kläglich und
she came from under up so plaintive and

hilfeflehend. Moni legte sich auf den Boden und
pleading for help Moni put himself on the ground and

beugte sich vor. Dort unten bewegte sich
bowed himself before There under moved itself

etwas. Jetzt sah er's deutlich, tief unten hing das
something Now saw he it clearly deep under hung the

Mäggerli an einem Ast, der aus dem Felsen
Mäggerli on a branch which from the rocks

herauskam, und winselte zum Erbarmen. Es mußte
came out and whimpered to the arouse pity It must
pitiful

hinuntergefallen sein.
to-under-fallen be
fallen down

Glücklicherweise hatte der Ast es aufgehalten,
Fortunately had the branch it held up

sonst hätte es in den Abgrund stürzen müssen.
otherwise had it in the chasm fall must

Aber auch noch jetzt, wenn es sich nicht mehr
But also still now when it himself not (any)more

an dem Ast festhalten konnte, mußte es auf der
on the branch firm hold could must it on the

Stelle in die Tiefe stürzen und sich das Genick
spot in the depth fall and itself the neck

brechen. In höchster Angst rief er hinunter: "Halt
break In highest fear called he down Hold

fest, Mäggerli, halt fest am Ast! Sieh, ich
firm Mäggerli hold firm to the branch Look I

komme schon und hole dich!" Aber wie sollte er
come already and get you But how should he

dahin gelangen? Die Felswand war so steil hier,
there to reach The rock-wall was so steep here

unmöglich konnte er da hinunterkommen, das
impossible could he there to-under-come that
down under come

sah Moni wohl ein. Aber das Geißlein mußte da
saw Moni well in But the little kid must there

unten etwa in der Höhe vom Regenfelsen sein,
under about in the height from the rain-rock be

dem überhängenden Gestein, unter das man
the overhanging rock under which one

sich beim Regen so gut flüchten konnte. Dort
himself at the rain so good flee could There
shelter

brachten die Geißbuben schon immer ihre
carried the goat boys already always their
(brachten zu; spent)

Tage bei schlechtem Wetter zu, darum hieß
days at bad weather to therefore was called

das Gestein schon von alter Zeit her der
the rock already from old time(s) since the

Regenfelsen. Von da aus, dachte Moni, konnte er
rain-rock From there out thought Moni could he

quer über den Felsen klettern und so mit dem
straight over the rocks climb and so with the

Zicklein zurückkommen.
kid come back

Schnell pfiff er die Herde zusammen und
Fast whistled he the herd together and

stieg mit ihr hinunter, bis zu der Stelle, wo es
rose with her down until to the spot where it
descended with it

zum Regenfelsen hineinging. Da ließ er sie
to the rain-rock went in There left he them

weiden und ging dem Felsen zu. Hier sah er auch
pasture and went the rocks to here saw he also

gleich, noch ein gutes Stück über sich, den
immediately still a good piece over himself the
long

Ast, an den sich das Geißlein klammerte. Er
branch on which himself the kid clung he

sah, daß es nicht leicht sei, da hinaufzuklettern
saw that it not easy be there up to climb
not would be easy

und mit dem Mäggerli auf dem Rücken wieder
and with the Mäggerli on the back again

hinunter. Aber anders war das Tierlein nicht zu
down But otherwise was the little animal not to

retten. Er dachte auch, der liebe Gott würde ihm
save He thought also the dear god would him

gewiß beistehen, dann könnte es ihm gelingen. Er
certainly stand by then could it him succeed He

faltete seine Hände, schaute zum Himmel auf und
folded his hands looked to the sky up and

betete: "Ach lieber Gott, hilf mir doch, daß ich das
prayed Oh dear god help me indeed that I the

Mäggerli erretten kann!" Jetzt war er voller
Mäggerli save can Now was he full

Vertrauen, daß alles gutgehen werde, und
(of) trust that everything go well would and

eilig kletterte er den Felsen hinauf, bis er bei
hurriedly climbed he the rocks up until he at

dem Ast oben angelangt war. Hier klammerte er
the branch above arrived was Here clung he

sich fest an mit beiden Füßen, hob dann das
himself firmly on with both feet lifted then the

zitternde, wimmernde Tierlein auf seine Schultern
trembling whimpering little animal on his shoulders

und kletterte nun mit großer Sorgfalt hinunter. Als
and climbed now with great care down As

er aber nun wieder den sicheren Grasboden unter
he but now again the assured grassy ground under

den Füßen hatte und das erschrockene Geißlein
the feet had and the scared kid

gerettet sah, da war er so froh, daß er laut
rescued saw there was he so happy that he loud

danken mußte und in den Himmel hinaufrief: "O
thank must and in the sky up called Oh

lieber Gott, ich danke dir tausendmal, daß du
dear god I thank you (a) thousand time(s) that you

uns so geholfen hast! O wie sind wir beide so
us so helped have Oh how are we both so

froh darüber!" Dann setzte er sich noch ein
happy about it Then set he himself still a

wenig auf den Boden und streichelte das Zicklein,
little on the ground and petted the kid

das immer noch an allen seinen zarten Gliedern
which always still on all its thin members
legs

zitterte, und tröstete es über die ausgestandene
trembled and comforted it over the stood out

Angst.
fear

Als wenig später Zeit zum Aufbruch war, setzte
As little later (it) time to the breaking up was set

Moni das Zicklein noch einmal auf seine Schultern
Moni the kid still once on his shoulders

und sagte fürsorglich: "Komm, du armes Mäggerli,
and said caring Come you poor Mäggerli

du zitterst ja immer noch. Heute kannst du nicht
you tremble yes always still Today can you not

heimgehen, ich muß dich tragen." Und so trug er
go home I must you carry And so carried he

das Tierlein, das sich fest an ihn schmiegte,
the little animal which itself firmly on him snuggled

den ganzen Weg hinunter.
the whole way down

Paula stand jetzt auf der letzten Anhöhe vor dem
Paula stood now on the last hill before the

Badehaus und erwartete den Geißbuben. Auch ihre
bathhouse and awaited the goatboy Also her
hotel

Tante hatte sie begleitet. Als nun Moni mit seiner
aunt had her accompanied As now Moni with his

Last auf dem Rücken herankam, wollte Paula
load on the back approached wanted Paula

wissen, ob das Zicklein krank sei, und zeigte
know whether the kid sick be and showed

große Teilnahme. Als Moni das sah, setzte er
great participation As Moni that saw set he
interest

sich gleich auf den Boden vor Paula hin
himself immediately on the ground before Paula -away-

und erzählte ihr sein heutiges Erlebnis mit dem
and told her his today's happening with the

Mäggerli.
Mäggerli

Das Fräulein nahm sehr lebhaften Anteil an der
The miss took very lively part on the

Sache und streichelte das gerettete Tierlein. Jetzt
thing and petted the saved little animal Now

lag es ruhig auf Monis Knien und sah sehr zierlich
lay it calm on Moni's knees and saw very elegant

aus mit seinen weißen Füßen und dem schönen
out with its white feet and the beautiful

schwarzen Pelzchen über dem Rücken. Es ließ sich
black little fur over the back It let itself

ganz     gern ein wenig streicheln.
completely gladly  a    little     stroke

"Jetzt singst du mir auch noch dein Lied, wenn
Now  sing  you  me  also  still  your  song  when

du schon einmal hier bist", sagte Paula. Moni war
you already  once  here  are  said  Paula  Moni  was

so fröhlich gestimmt, daß er gern aus voller Brust
so  merrily  at mood  that  he  gladly  out  (of) full  breast

anstimmte und sein ganzes Lied bis zu Ende sang.
toned in  and  his  whole  song  until  to  end  sang

Das gefiel der Paula ausnehmend gut, und sie
That pleased  the  Paula  exceptionally  well  and  she

sagte, er müsse es ihr
said  he  must  it  her

noch    öfter    singen. Dann zog die ganze
still  more often  sing    Then  drew  the  whole

Gesellschaft zusammen zum
company    together  to the

Badehaus hinunter. Hier wurde das Zicklein auf
bathhouse down Here became the kid on
hotel

sein Lager gelegt, und
its bed laid and

Moni nahm Abschied. Paula ging in ihr Zimmer
Moni took leave Paula went in her room

zurück, um hier der
back for here the

Tante noch lange von dem Geißbuben zu erzählen,
aunt still long from the goat boy to tell
about

auf dessen fröhlichen
on whose joyful

Morgengesang sie sich schon jetzt wieder freute.
morning song she herself already now again pleased

# Ein Besuch
## *A Visit*

So waren mehrere Tage vergangen, einer so sonnig
So were multiple days gone by one so sunny

und klar wie der andere, denn es war ein
and clear as the other then it was a

besonders schöner Sommer. Und der Himmel
particularly beautiful summer And the sky

blieb blau und wolkenlos vom Morgen bis
remained blue and cloudless from the morning until

zum Abend.
to the evening

Jeden Morgen in der Frühe war der Geißbub
Every morning in the early (hour) was the goat boy

mit hellem Gesang am Badehaus vorbeigezogen,
with bright singing at the bathhouse pulled past
hotel

| jeden | Abend | mit | hellem | Gesang | wieder |
|---|---|---|---|---|---|
| every | evening | with | clear | singing | again |

| zurückgekehrt. | Und | alle | Badegäste | waren | so |
|---|---|---|---|---|---|
| returned | And | all | (the) bathing guests | were | so |
| | | | the hotel guests | | |

| an | das | fröhliche | Singen | gewöhnt, | daß | keiner | es |
|---|---|---|---|---|---|---|---|
| on | that | happy | singing | used | that | none | it |

| hätte | missen | mögen. |
|---|---|---|
| had | miss | may |

| Vor | allen | aber | freute | sich | Paula | an | Monis |
|---|---|---|---|---|---|---|---|
| Before | all | however | enjoyed | herself | Paula | on | Moni's |

| Fröhlichkeit | und | ging | ihm | fast | jeden | Abend |
|---|---|---|---|---|---|---|
| happiness | and | went | him | almost | every | evening |

| entgegen, | um | ein | Gespräch | mit | ihm | anzuknüpfen. |
|---|---|---|---|---|---|---|
| towards | for | a | conversation | with | him | to tie up |

| An | einem | sonnigen | Morgen | war | Moni | wieder | oben |
|---|---|---|---|---|---|---|---|
| On | a | sunny | morning | was | Moni | again | above |

| bei | der | Felsenkanzel | angelangt | und | wollte | sich |
|---|---|---|---|---|---|---|
| at | the | rock-pulpit | arrived | and | wanted | himself |

eben auf den Boden setzen, als er sich noch
just on the ground set as he himself still

anders besann. "Nein, vorwärts! Ihr habt ja das
different re-thought No further You have yes the
indeed

letztemal die guten Blättlein alle stehenlassen
last time the good little leaves all stand let

müssen, weil wir dem Mäggerli helfen mußten,
must because we the Mäggerli help must

jetzt geht's noch einmal hinauf, da könnt ihr
now goes it still once up there can you

fertig nagen!" Und mit Freuden sprangen ihm die
ready gnaw And with joy jumped him the

Geißen alle nach, denn sie merkten, daß es zu
goats all after then she noticed that it to

den schönen Büschen an den Drachensteinen
the beautiful shrubs on the dragon stones

hinauf ging. Diesmal hielt Moni aber sein kleines
up went This time held Moni however his little

Mäggerli die ganze Zeit im Arm fest, riß ihm
Mäggerli the whole time in the arm firmly ripped him

die guten Blättlein selber ab und ließ es aus
the good little leaf self off and let it from

seiner Hand fressen. Das gefiel dem Geißlein am
his hand eat That pleased the kid goat at the

allerbesten, es rieb ganz vergnügt von Zeit zu
very best it rubbed completely pleased from time to

Zeit sein Köpfchen an Monis Schulter und
time its little head on Moni's shoulder and

meckerte fröhlich. So war der ganze Morgen
bleated merrily So was the whole morning

vergangen und Moni merkte erst an seinem
gone away and Moni noticed only on his

Hunger, daß es spät geworden war. Er hatte
hunger that it late become was He had

aber sein Essen unten bei der Felsenkanzel in
however his food under at the rock-pulpit in

der   kleinen   Höhle   hegen   lassen,   da   er
the   small   hollow   harbor   let   there   he

mittags   wieder   hinunter   kommen   wollte.
in the afternoon   again   down   come   wanted

"So,   ihr   habt   nun   schon   viel   Gutes   bekommen,
So   you   have   now   already   much   good   become

und   ich   habe   noch   gar   nichts",   sagte   er   zu   seinen
and   I   have   still   at all   nothing   said   he   to   his

Geißen.   "Jetzt   muß   ich   auch   etwas   haben   und
goats   Now   must   I   also   something   have   and

unten   findet   ihr   noch   genug,   kommt!"   Dann   pfiff
under   find   you   still   enough   come   Then   whistled

er   laut,   und   die   ganze   Schar   zog   auf   und   davon,
he   loud   and   the   whole   herd   drew   up   and   there-from

die   lebhaftesten   immer   voran   und   allen   voraus   die
the   liveliest   always   in front   and   all   in front   the

leichtfüßige   Schwalbe,   der   heute   etwas
light footed   Swallow   who   today   something

Unerwartetes begegnen sollte. Sie sprang hinunter
unexpected to meet should She jumped down

von Stein zu Stein und über manche Felsspalte
from stone to stone and over many rock cracks

weg, aber auf einmal konnte sie nicht weiter.
away but at once could she not further

Unmittelbar vor ihr stand ganz plötzlich eine
Immediately before her stood completely suddenly a

Gemse und schaute ihr neugierig ins Gesicht.
chamois and looked her curious in the face
mountain sheep

Das war der Schwalbe noch nicht vorgekommen.
That was the swallow still not occurred

Sie stand da, schaute die Fremde fragend an
She stood there looked the stranger questioning on

und wartete, daß ihr diese aus dem Weg gehe.
and waited that her this out the way go
this one out of her

Denn sie wollte auf den Felsblock springen, der
Then she wanted on the rock-block jump which

vor ihr aufragte. Aber die Gemse rührte
before her rose up However the chamois stirred
mountain sheep

sich nicht und schaute der Schwalbe frech ins
itself not and looked the Swallow fresh in the
cheeky

Gesicht. So standen beide voreinander, immer
face so stood both in front of each other always

hartnäckiger, und noch heute würden sie dort
more stubborn and still today would they there

stehen, wenn nicht inzwischen der große Sultan
stand when not in the meantime the great Sultan

herbeigekommen wäre. Sofort erkannte er die
there by come would be Immediately recognized he the

Sachlage und kletterte vorsichtig an der Schwalbe
situation and climbed carefully on the Swallow

vorbei. Plötzlich stieß er die Gemse so weit
past Suddenly bumped he the chamois so far
mountain sheep

und so gewaltig auf die Seite, daß sie einen
and so enormously on the side that she a

kühnen Sprung machen mußte, um nicht über die
daring jump make must for not over the

Felsen hinabzurutschen.
rocks away down to slide

Die Schwalbe aber zog triumphierend ihres
The Swallow however pulled triumphantly her
continued

Weges, und der Sultan schritt befriedigt und stolz
road and the Sultan stepped satisfied and proud

hinter ihr her, denn er fühlte sich als sicherer
behind her away then he felt himself as sure

Beschützer seiner Herde. Inzwischen war von
defender of his herd In the meantime was from

oben herab Moni und von unten herauf ein
above down Moni and from under up an

anderer Geißbub auf einem nahen Platz
other goat boy on a close place

angekommen und blickten auch erstaunt einander
arrived and looked also astonished each other

an. Aber sie kannten sich, und nach der ersten
on But they knew each other and after the first

Überraschung begrüßten sie sich freundlich.
surprise greeted they each other friendly

Es war der Jörgli von Küblis, der schon den
It was -the- Jörgli from Küblis who already the

halben Morgen lang vergebens den Moni gesucht
half morning long in vain the Moni sought

hatte und ihn nun hier oben traf, wo er
had and him now here above encountered where he

ihn gar nicht mehr vermutete.
him at all not (any)more guessed

"Ich habe nicht gedacht, daß du so hoch
I have not thought that you so high

hinaufgehen würdest mit den Geißen", sagte der
go up would with the goats said the

Jörgli.
Jörgli

"Freilich gehe ich", entgegnete Moni, "aber nicht
Freely / Indeed — go — I — replied — Moni — but — not

immer. Gewöhnlich bin ich bei der Felsenkanzel.
always — Usually — am — I — at — the — rock-pulpit

Warum bist du da heraufgekommen?"
Why — are — you — then — up come

"Ich will dir einen Besuch machen", war die
I — want — you — a — visit — make — was — the

Antwort, "ich habe dir allerhand zu erzählen. Auch
answer — I — have — you — all sorts — to — tell — Also

habe ich hier zwei Geißen, die bringe ich dem
have — I — here — two — goats — those — bring — I — the

Wirt im Bad, er will eine kaufen, und da
host — in the / hotel — bath — he — wants — one — buy — and — there

dachte ich, ich wollte noch zu dir hinauf."
thought — I — I — wanted — still — to — you — up

"Sind es deine Geißen?" fragte Moni.
Are — it / they — your — goats — asked — Moni

"Natürlich, die fremden habe ich nicht zu
Of course the strange (goats) have I not to

hüten, ich bin nicht mehr Geißbub."
look after I am not (any)more goat boy

Darüber mußte sich Moni sehr wundern, denn
There-about must himself Moni much wonder then

zu gleicher Zeit mit ihm war der Jörgli Geißbub
at similar time with him was the Jörgli goat boy

von Küblis geworden, und Moni begriff nicht,
from Küblis become and Moni understood not

daß das so aufhören konnte und der Jörgli nicht
that that so stop could and the Jörgli not

einmal jammerte.
once wailed
even complained

Inzwischen waren Hirten und Geißen bei der
In the meantime were shepherds and goats at the

Felsenkanzel angekommen. Moni holte Brot und ein
rock-pulpit arrived Moni got bread and a

Stückchen getrocknetes Fleisch hervor und lud
bit of dried meat forth and loaded
invited

den Jörgli zum Mittagessen ein. Sie setzten
the Jörgli to the lunch in They set

sich beide auf die Kanzel hinaus und ließen
themselves both on the pulpit out and let

sich's gut schmecken. Denn es war sehr spät
itself it good taste Then it was very late

geworden, und sie hatten beide ausgezeichneten
become and they had both excellent
enormous

Appetit. Als nun alles aufgegessen und dann
apetite As now everything eaten up and then

noch ein wenig Geißmilch getrunken worden war,
still a little goat milk drunk become was

legte sich der Jörgli ganz behaglich der Länge
put himself the Jörgli completely cosily the length

nach auf den Boden und stützte seinen Kopf auf
after on the ground and supported his head on

beide Ellbogen. Moni aber war sitzen geblieben,
both elbows Moni but was sit remained

denn er schaute immer gern von oben in das tiefe
then he looked always gladly from above in the deep

Tal hinunter.
valley down

"Was bist du denn jetzt, Jörgli, wenn du nicht
What are you then now Jörgli when you not

mehr Geißbub bist?" fing Moni nun an,
(any)more goat boy are caught Moni now on
started

"etwas mußt du doch sein."
something must you indeed be

"Freilich bin ich etwas und etwas Rechtes",
Indeed am I something and something true

erwiderte Jörgli, "Eierbub bin ich. Jeden Tag gehe
answered Jörgli Egg boy am I Every day go

ich mit den Eiern in alle Wirtshäuser, so weit ich
I with the eggs in all (the) inns so far I

komme. Hier hinauf ins Badehaus komme ich
come Here up in the bathhouse come I
hotel

auch, gestern war ich schon dort."
also yesterday was I already there

Moni schüttelte den Kopf: "Das ist nichts, Eierbub
Moni shook the head That is nothing egg boy

möchte ich nicht sein, tausendmal lieber will ich
may I not be thousand time(s) rather want I

Geißbub sein, das ist viel schöner."
goat boy be that is much more beautiful

"Ja warum denn?"
yes why then

"Die Eier sind ja nicht lebendig, mit denen kannst
The eggs are yes not alive with which can

du kein Wort reden. Und sie laufen dir nicht
you no word talk And they run you not

nach wie die Geißen, die sich freuen, wenn
after as the goats who themselves enjoy when

du kommst und anhänglich sind und jedes Wort
you come and affectionate are and each word

verstehen, das du mit ihnen redest. Du kannst
understand that you with them talk You can

keine Freude mit deinen Eiern haben wie mit den
no joy with your eggs have as with the

Geißen hier oben."
goats here above

"Ja und du", unterbrach ihn Jörgli, "was hast du
es and you interrupted him Jörgli what have you

denn für große Freuden hier oben? Jetzt hast du
then for great joy here above Now have you

wohl sechsmal aufstehen müssen, während wir
well six times get up must while we

beim Essen waren, nur wegen des dummen
at the food were only because of of the dumb

Geißleins, damit es nicht hinunterfällt. Ist denn
little goats there-with it not falls down Is then

das  eine  Freude?"
that   a      joy


"Ja,   das   tue   ich   ganz   gern.   Nicht   wahr,
Yes   that   do    I    completely   gladly   Not   true


Mäggerli,  komm!  Komm!"  Moni  sprang  auf  und  lief
Mäggerli    come    Come    Moni   jumped   up   and   ran


dem  Geißlein  nach,  denn  es  machte   ganz
the   little goat   after   then   it   made   completely


unvorsichtige  Freudensprünge.  Als  er  wieder  saß,
careless        jumps of joy      As   he   again    sat


sagte  Jörgli:  "Es  gibt  auch  ein  anderes  Mittel,  die
said   Jörgli    It   gives   also   an   other   means   the


jungen  Geißen  zu  halten,  daß  sie  nicht  über  die
young   goats   to   hold   that   they   not   over   the


Felsen  hinabfallen  und  man  ihnen  nicht  immer
rocks    fall down    and   one   them   not   always


nachspringen  muß  wie  du."
after jump      must   like   you

"Was für eins?" fragte Moni.
What for one asked moni

"Man steckt einen Stecken fest in den Boden und
One sticks a stick firmly in the ground and

bindet die Geiß mit einem Bein daran. Sie zappelt
binds the goat with one leg there-on She fidgets

dann zwar furchtbar, aber sie kann doch nicht
then indeed terribly but she can indeed not

fort."
away

"Du wirst doch nicht glauben, daß ich so etwas
You will indeed not believe that I so something

mit dem Geißlein mache", sagte der Moni ganz
with the little goat do said the Moni completely

entrüstet. Er zog das Mäggerli zu sich und hielt
indignant He pulled the Mäggerli to himself and held

es fest, als müßte er es schützen.
it firmly as must he it protect

"Um das Geißlein mußt du dich nicht mehr
For the kid must you yourself not (any)more

lange sorgen", fing Jörgli wieder an, "das kommt
long worry caught Jörgli again on that comes

nicht mehr hier herauf."
not (any)more here up

"Was? Was? Was sagst du, Jörgli?" fuhr Moni auf.
What What What say you Jörgli drove Moni up
started

"Pah, weißt du's denn nicht? Der Wirt will es
Pah know you it then not The host wants it

nicht aufziehen, es ist ihm zu schwach, es wird
not pull up it is him too weak it becomes
raise

nie eine kräftige Geiß. Er hat es meinem Vater
never a strong goat He has it my father

verkaufen wollen, aber der wollte es auch nicht.
sell want but that one wanted it also not

Nun will es der Wirt nächste Woche schlachten,
Now wants it the host next week butcher

und dann kauft er unseren Scheck dort."
and then buys he our check there

Moni war vor Schrecken ganz weiß geworden.
Moni was before fright completely white become
of

Erst konnte er kein Wort sagen, aber jetzt
First could he no word say but now

jammerte er laut und rief:
wailed he loud and called

"Nein, nein, das dürfen sie nicht tun, Mäggerli,
No no that may they not do Mäggerli

das dürfen sie nicht tun. Sie dürfen dich nicht
that may they not do They may you not

schlachten, das kann ich nicht ertragen. Oh, ich
butcher that can I not endure Oh I

will lieber gleich mit dir sterben. Nein, das
want rather immediately with you die No that

kann ja nicht sein!"
can indeed not be

"Tu doch nicht so", sagte Jörgli ärgerlich und zog
Do indeed not so said Jörgli annoyed and pulled

den Moni in die Höhe, der sich in seinem
the Moni in the height who himself in his

Jammer mit dem Gesicht zu Boden geworfen hatte.
misery with the face to ground thrown had

"Steh doch auf, du weißt ja, daß das Geißlein
Stand indeed up you know well that the kid

nun einmal dem Wirt gehört und er damit
now once the host heard and he there-with
belonged

machen darf, was er will. Denk doch nicht
do may what he wants Think indeed not

mehr dran! Komm ich weiß noch etwas:
(any)more there-on Come I know still something

Sieh! Sieh!" Dann hielt Jörgli dem Moni die eine
Look Look Then held Jörgli the Moni the one

Hand hin, und mit der anderen deckte er den
hand away and with the other covered he the

Gegenstand fast zu, den Moni bewundern sollte.
object almost to that Moni admire should

Es funkelte aber ganz wunderbar aus der Hand
It sparkled but completely wonderful from the hand

heraus, denn die Sonne blitzte eben dort hinein.
out then the sun flashed just there inside

"Was ist's?" fragte Moni, als es eben wieder
What is it asked Moni as it just again

aufblitzte, von einem Sonnenstrahl beleuchtet.
flashed up from a sunbeam illuminated

"Rat!"
Guess

"Ein Ring?"
A ring

"Nein, aber so etwas Ähnliches."
No but so something similar

"Wer hat dir's gegeben?"
Who has yourself it given

"Gegeben? Niemand, ich hab es selbst gefunden."
Given Nobody I have it myself found

"Dann gehört es aber nicht dir, Jörgli."
Then belongs it however not you Jörgli

"Warum nicht? Ich habe es niemand genommen,
Why not I have it nobody taken (from)

ich wäre fast mit dem Fuß darauf getreten,
I would be almost with the foot thereupon stepped
become

dann wär's doch zerbrochen. Ich kann es ebenso
then was it indeed broken I can it likewise

gut behalten."
well keep

"Wo hast du's gefunden?"
Where have you it found

"Unten beim Badehaus, gestern abend."
Under at the bathhouse yesterday evening
hotel

"Dann hat es jemand aus dem Haus unten
Then has it someone from the house under

verloren. Du mußt es dem Wirt sagen, und wenn
lost   You   must   it   the   host   say   and   when

du's nicht tust, so tue ich's heute Abend."
you it   not   do   so   do   I it   today   evening

"Nein, nein, Moni, tue nur das nicht", sagte Jörgli
No   no   Moni   do   only   that   not   said   Jörgli

jetzt bittend, "sieh, ich will dir zeigen, was es ist.
now   pleading   look   I   want you   show   what   it   is

Und ich will es in einen von den Wirtshäusern an
And   I   want   it   in   one   of   the   inns   to

ein Zimmermädchen verkaufen, sie muß mir aber
a   room-maid   sell   she   must   me   however

vier Franken geben, dann geb ich dir auch einen
four   franks   give   then   give   I   you   also   one
      (money)

oder zwei, und dann weiß ja niemand etwas
or   two   and   then   knows   yes   nobody   something

davon."
there-from

"Ich will nichts! Ich will nichts!" unterbrach ihn
I want nothing I want nothing interrupted him

Moni heftig, "und der liebe Gott hat alles
Moni vehemently and the dear god has everything

gehört, was du gesagt hast."
heard what you said have

Jörgli schaute zum Himmel auf. "Ja, so weit weg",
Jörgli looked at the sky up Yes so far away

sagte er zweifelhaft. Er fing aber gleich an,
said he doubtful He caught however immediately -on-
started

leiser zu reden.
quieter to talk

"Er hört dich doch", sagte Moni zuversichtlich.
He hears you indeed said Moni confidentially

Dem Jörgli war es nicht mehr recht wohl in
The Jörgli was it not (any)more right well in

seiner Haut. Wenn er nur den Moni auf seine
his skin When he only the Moni on his

Seite zu bringen wußte, sonst war alles
side to bring knew otherwise was everything

verloren. Er dachte lange nach. "Moni", sagte er
lost He thought long after Moni said he

plötzlich, "ich will dir etwas versprechen, das
suddenly I want you something promise that

dich freut, wenn du keinem Menschen etwas
you pleases when you no people something

von dem Gefundenen sagen willst. Du brauchst ja
from the found (object) say want You need yes

auch nichts davon zu nehmen, dann hast du
also nothing there-from to take then have you

nichts damit zu tun. Wenn du das willst, so
nothing there-with to do When you that wants so

will ich dafür sorgen, daß mein Vater doch das
want I therefore care that my father indeed the
take care

Mäggerli kauft. Dann wird es nicht geschlachtet,
Mäggerli buys Then becomes it not butchered

willst  du?"
want  you


In  Moni  entstand  ein  harter  Kampf.  Es  war  ein
In  Moni  arose  a  hard  fight  It  was  a


Unrecht,  wenn  er  dabei  half,  den  Fund  zu
wrong  when  he  there-by  helped  the  find  to


verheimlichen.  Jörgli  hatte  seine  Hand  aufgemacht,
conceal  Jörgli  had  his  hand  opened


es  lag  ein  Kreuz  darin,  mit  vielen  Steinen  besetzt,
it  lay  a  cross  therein  with  many  stones  occupied
there


die  in  allen  Farben  funkelten.  Moni  sah  wohl,  daß
which  in  all  colors  sparkled  Moni  saw  well  that


das  nicht  ein  wertloses  Ding  war,  nach  dem
that  not  a  worthless  thing  was  after  which


niemand  fragen  werde.  Wenn  er  schweigen  würde,
nobody  ask  would  When  he  silent be  would


würde  er  etwas  behalten,  was  ihm  nicht
would  he  something  keep  what  him  not

gehörte. Aber auf der anderen Seite war das
belonged to But on the other side was the

kleine, liebevolle Mäggerli, das sollte auf
little dear Mäggerli that should on
in

schreckliche Weise mit einem Messer getötet
(a) horrible manner with a knife killed

werden, und er konnte das verhindern, wenn er
become and he could that prevent when he

schweigen wollte. Eben jetzt lag das Geißlein so
to be silent wanted Just now lay the little goat so

vertrauensvoll neben ihm, als wußte es, daß er
trustful beside him as knew it that he

ihm immer helfen wurde. Nein, er konnte es nicht
him always help would No he could it not

geschehen lassen, er mußte es retten.
happen let he must it save

"Einverstanden, Jörgli", sagte er, aber ohne
Agreed Jörgli said he but without

Freudigkeit.
joy

"So schlag ein." Und Jörgli hielt Moni seine Hand
So hit in And Jörgli held Moni his hand

hin, daß er hinein verspreche, denn nur so galt
to that he inside promise then only so counted

ein Versprechen unwiderruflich.
a promise (as) irrevocable

Jörgli war sehr froh, daß er nun seiner Sache
Jörgli was very happy that he now his affair

sicher war. Da aber Moni so still geworden
sure was There however Moni so quiet become

war und er einen viel weiteren Weg nach Hause
was and he a much further way to house

hatte als Moni, so beschloß er, mit seinen zwei
had as Moni so decided he with his two

Geißen aufzubrechen. Er verabschiedete sich von
goats to break up He took leave himself from

Moni und pfiff den beiden Gefährten, die
Moni and whistled the both companions who

sich inzwischen zu den weidenden Geißen
themselves in the meantime to the pasturing goats

des Moni gesellt hatten. Es hatten einige
of the Moni joined had It had some

bedenkliche Angriffe zwischen den beiden Parteien
serious attacks between the both parties

stattgefunden, denn die Fideriser Geißen wußten
place found then the from Fideris goats knew

nicht, daß man mit einem Besuch artig sein muß.
not that one with a visit good be must

Und die Kübliser Geißen wußten nicht, daß man
And the from Küblis goats knew not that one

nicht gleich die besten Kräutlein aussuchen und
not immediately the best little herbs select and

die anderen davon wegdrücken darf, wenn man
the others there-from force away may when one

auf Besuch ist. Als nun der Jörgli ein Stück den
on   visit   is   As  now  the  Jörgli   a    bit   the

Berg    hinuntergegangen  war, brach  auch  Moni
mountain    down gone      was  broke  also  Moni

mit  seiner  Schar  auf, aber  er  war   ganz     still
with  his    herd    up   but   he  was  completely  quiet

und  sang  keinen  Ton  und  tat  keinen  Pfiff   auf
and  sang   no     tune  and  did   no    whistle   on

dem  ganzen  Heimweg.
the   whole   way home

# Moni kann nicht mehr singen
## *Moni Can Not (Any)More Sing*

Moni   kam   am   folgenden   Morgen   genauso   still
Moni   came   at the   following   morning   just as   quiet

und   niedergeschlagen   wie   am   Abend   vorher   den
and   cast down   as   at the   evening   before   the

Weg   zum   Badehaus   daher.   Leise   holte   er   die
way   to the   bathhouse   there-from   Softly   got   he   the
   hotel

Geißen   des   Wirts   heraus   und   stieg   weiter
goats   from the   innkeper   out   and   climbed   further

hinauf,   aber   er   sang   keinen   Ton,   er   schickte
up   but   he   sang   no   tune   he   sent

keinen   Jodel   in   die   Luft   hinauf.   Er   ließ   seinen
no   yodel   in   the   air   up   He   let   his

Kopf   hängen   und   machte   ein   Gesicht,   als   fürchtete
head   hang   and   made   a   face   as   feared

er sich vor etwas. Hier und da blickte er
he himself before something Here and there looked he

auch scheu um sich, ob ihm nicht jemand
also fearful around himself whether him not someone

nachkomme und ihn etwas fragen wolle.
come after and him something ask wanted

Moni konnte gar nicht mehr lustig sein. Er
Moni could at all not (any)more merry be He

wußte erst selbst nicht so recht, warum? Er wollte
knew first himself not so right why He wanted

sich freuen, daß er das Mäggerli gerettet hatte
himself enjoy that he the Mäggerli rescued had

und einmal singen, aber er brachte nichts heraus.
and once sing but he brought nothing out

Der Himmel war heute mit Wolken bedeckt, und
The sky was today with clouds covered and

Moni dachte, wenn die Sonne komme, würde er
Moni thought when the sun come would he

schon  wieder  lustiger  werden.
already  again  merry  become (would)

Als  er  oben  angekommen  war,  fing  es  ganz
As  he  above  arrived  was  caught  it  completely
started

tüchtig  zu  regnen  an.  Er  flüchtete  unter  den
thoroughly  to  rain  -on-  He  fled  under  the

Regenfelsen,  denn  es  goß  bald  in  Strömen  vom
rain-rock  then  it  poured  soon  in  streams  from the

Himmel  herunter.
sky  down

Die  Geißen  kamen  auch  heran  und  stellten
The  goats  came  also  near  and  put

sich  da  und  dort  unter  die  Felsen.  Die
themselves  there  and  there  under  the  rocks  The

vornehme  Schwarze  hatte  gleich  ihren  schönen
distinguished  black (one)  had  immediately  her  beautiful

glänzenden  Pelz  schonen  wollen  und  war  noch
shining  fur  spare  want  and  was  still

vor dem Moni unter den Felsen gekrochen. Sie
before the Moni under the rocks crept (up) She

saß jetzt hinter dem Moni und schaute aus dem
sat now behind the Moni and looked from the

behaglichen Winkel vergnügt in den strömenden
comfortable corner pleased in the streaming

Regen hinaus. Das Mäggerli stand vor seinem
rain out The Mäggerli stood before his

Beschützer unter dem vorragenden Felsen und
defender under the uprising rocks and

rieb zärtlich sein Köpfchen an seinem Knie. Und
rubbed tender his little head on his knees And

dann schaute es erstaunt zu ihm auf, denn Moni
then looked it astonished to him up then Moni

sagte kein Wort, das war das Zicklein nicht
said no word that was the kid not

gewohnt. Auch seine Braune scharrte zu seinen
used Also his brown (one) pawed at his

Füßen und meckerte, denn er hatte den ganzen
feet and bleated then he had the whole

Morgen noch nichts zu ihr gesagt. Moni saß
morning still nothing to her said Moni sat

nachdenklich da. Er hatte sich auf seinen
thoughtful there He had himself on his

Stecken gestützt, den er bei solchem Wetter
stick supported which he at such weather

immer zur Hand nahm, damit er an den steilen
always to the hand took there-with he on the steep

Stellen nicht ausrutschen konnte. Denn an
places not out-slide could Then on
slip

Regentagen zog er Schuhe an. Jetzt, da Moni
rain-days pulled he shoes on Now there Moni

stundenlang unter dem Regenfelsen saß, hatte er
hours long under the rain-rock sat had he

Zeit zum Nachdenken.
time for the pondering

Jetzt überdachte Moni, was er dem Jörgli
Now thought over Moni what he the Jörgli

versprochen hatte. Und es kam ihm nun nicht
promised had And it came him now not

anders vor, als ob der Jörgli etwas
different before as whether the Jörgli something

genommen habe und er selbst dasselbe tue.
taken have and he himself the same do

Schließlich hatte ihm der Jörgli doch auch etwas
Finally had him the Jörgli indeed also something

für sein Schweigen gegeben. Er hatte etwas
for his silence given He had something

getan, was unrecht war, und der liebe Gott war
done what wrong was and the dear god was

jetzt gegen ihn, das fühlte er in seinem Herzen. Es
now against him that felt he in his heart It

war ihm recht, daß es dunkel war und regnete
was him right that it dark was and rained

und er unter dem Felsen verborgen war. Denn er
and he under the rocks concealed was Then he

hätte doch nicht wie sonst in den blauen
had indeed not as otherwise in the blue

Himmel hinaufsehen dürfen, er fürchtete sich
sky up see may he feared himself

jetzt vor dem lieben Gott. Aber auch noch
now before the dear god But also still

andere Dinge mußte Moni denken. Wenn nun
other things must Moni think When now

wieder das Mäggerli über einen steilen Felsen
again the Mäggerli over a steep rock

hinunterfiele, und er wollte es holen, und der liebe
fall down and he wanted it to get and the dear

Gott würde ihn nicht mehr beschützen, wenn er
god would him not (any)more protect when he

auch nicht mehr zu ihm beten und rufen dürfte,
also not (any)more to him pray and call might

dann hätte er keine Sicherheit mehr. Und wenn
then had he no security (any)more And when

er dann ausrutschte und mit dem Mäggerli tief
he then slipped and with the Mäggerli deep

über die zackigen Felsen hinunterfiele und beide
over the jagged rocks down fell and both

ganz zerrissen und zerschmettert unten im
completely torn up and crushed under in the

Abgrund lägen...
chasm lay

O nein, sprach er ängstlich zu sich, so durfte es
Oh no spoke he fearfully to himself so may it

doch nicht kommen. Er mußte dafür sorgen,
indeed not come He must therefore (take) care
be

daß er wieder beten und vor den lieben Gott
that he again pray and before the dear god

kommen konnte mit allem, was ihm auf dem
come could with all what him on the

Herzen lag. Dann konnte er auch wieder fröhlich
heart lay Then could he also again merrily

sein, das fühlte Moni. Er wollte sich von der
be that felt Moni He wanted himself from the

Last befreien, die ihn bedrückte, er wollte gehen
load free that him pressed he wanted to go

und alles dem Wirt sagen —aber dann?
and everything the innkeeper say but then

Dann wurde Jörgli seinen Vater nicht überreden,
Then would Jörgli his father not persuade

und der Wirt würde das Mäggerli totstechen. O
and the innkeeper would the Mäggerli dead-stick Oh
                                        kill

nein! Das konnte er nicht aushalten, und er sagte:
no That could he not out-hold and he said
                              bear

"Nein, ich tue es nicht, ich sage nichts." Aber es
No I do it not I say nothing But it

war ihm nicht wohl dabei und sein schlechtes
was him not well there-by and his bad

Gewissen wurde immer größer.
conscious became always bigger

So verging dem Moni der ganze Tag. Er kehrte
So passed the Moni the whole day He turned

abends so lautlos heim, wie er morgens
in the evening so soundless home as he in the morning
as quiet

gekommen war. Und als unten beim Badehaus
come was And as under at the bathhouse
had hotel

Paula stand und schnell zum Geißenstall
Paula stood and fast to the goat-stable

herübersprang und teilnehmend fragte: "Moni, was
over jumped and interested asked Moni what
rushed over

fehlt dir? Warum singst du denn gar nicht
is wrong with you Why sing you then at all not

mehr?" —da wandte er sich scheu ab und sagte:
(any)more then turned he himself shy off and said

"Ich kann nicht." Und so schnell wie möglich
I can not And so fast as possible

**machte er sich mit seinen Geißen davon.**
made he himself with his goats there-from

**Paula sagte oben zu ihrer Tante: "Wenn ich**
Paul said up(stairs) to her aunt When I

**doch nur wußte, was der Geißbub hat, er ist ja**
indeed only knew what the goat boy has he is yes
indeed

**ganz verändert, man kennt ihn gar nicht**
completely changed one knows him at all not
recognizes

**mehr.**
(any)more

**Wenn er doch nur wieder sänge."**
When he indeed just again would sing

**"Es wird der schreckliche Regen sein, der den**
It will the horrible rain be which the

**Buben so verstimmt", meinte die Tante.**
boy so upsets thought the aunt

**"Nun kommt auch alles zusammen. Wir wollen**
Now comes also everything together We want

doch heimgehen, Tante", bat Paula, "das Vergnügen
indeed go home aunt bade Paula the pleasure

hier ist aus. Erst verliere ich mein schönes Kreuz,
here is out First lose I my beautiful cross
gone

und es ist nicht mehr zu finden. Dann kommt
and it is not (any)more to find Then comes

dieser endlose Regen, und nun kann man nicht
this endless rain and now can one not

einmal mehr den lustigen Geißbuben zuhören.
once (any)more the merry goat boy listen to
even

Wir wollen fort."
We want away

"Die Kur muß zu Ende gemacht werden, da
The cure must to end made become there
treatment

kann ich dir nicht helfen", erklärte die Tante.
can I you not help explained the aunt

Dunkel und grau war es auch am folgenden
dark and grey was it also at the following

Morgen, und der Regen strömte unausgesetzt
morning and the rain flowed incessantly

nieder. Moni brachte seinen Tag ebenso zu wie
down Moni brought his day likewise to as
went through

den vorhergegangenen. Er saß unter dem Felsen,
the before gone He sat under the rock

und seine Gedanken gingen ruhelos immer im
and his thoughts went restless always in the

Kreise herum. Immer wenn er zu sich sagte:
circle around Always when he to himself said

"Jetzt will ich gehen und das Unrecht gestehen,
Now want I go and the wrong confess

damit ich wieder zum lieben Gott aufsehen
there-with I again to the dear god see up

darf", da sah er wieder das Zicklein unter dem
may there saw he again the kid under the

Messer vor sich. Er dachte nach, und sein
knife before himself He thought -after- and his

| schlechtes | Gewissen | plagte | ihn | so | sehr, | daß | er |
|---|---|---|---|---|---|---|---|
| bad | conscious | plagued tortured | him | so | much | that | he |

| am | Abend | ganz | müde | war | und | im |
|---|---|---|---|---|---|---|
| at the | evening | completely | tired | was | and | in the |

| strömenden | Regen | heimschlich, | als | merkte | er |
|---|---|---|---|---|---|
| streaming | rain | away-snuck | as | noticed | he |

| nichts | davon. |
|---|---|
| nothing | there-from |

| Beim | Badehaus | stand | der | Wirt | in | der | Hintertür |
|---|---|---|---|---|---|---|---|
| At the | bathhouse hotel | stood | the | host innkeeper | in | the | back door |

| und | fuhr | den | Moni | an: | "Komm | einmal | mit | den |
|---|---|---|---|---|---|---|---|---|
| and | drove | the | Moni | on | come | once | with | the |

| Geißen | her, | sie | sind | naß | genug! | Was | kriechst | du |
|---|---|---|---|---|---|---|---|---|
| goats | here | they | are | wet | enough | What | crawl | you |

| auch | wie | eine | Schnecke | den | Berg | hinunter! | Ich |
|---|---|---|---|---|---|---|---|
| also | like | a | snail | the | mountain | down | I |

| wundere | mich | schon | die | ganze | Zeit | über | dich." |
|---|---|---|---|---|---|---|---|
| wonder | myself | already | the | whole | time | about | you |

So unfreundlich war der Wirt noch nie gewesen,

im Gegenteil, immer hatte er dem fröhlichen

Geißbuben die freundlichsten Worte zugerufen.

Aber Monis verändertes Wesen gefiel ihm nicht,

und dazu war er noch schlechter Laune, denn

Fräulein Paula hatte ihm ihren Verlust geklagt. Sie

hatte behauptet, das kostbare Kreuz könne nur

im Haus oder unmittelbar vor der Haustür

verloren gegangen sein. Denn sie sei an jenem Tag

nur herausgegangen, um abends den
only gone out for in the evening the

heimkehrenden Geißbuben singen zu hören. Daß
returning home goat boys sing to hear That

man aber sagen sollte, es könne in seinem Haus
one however say should it could in his house

ein so wertvolles Ding verloren gehen, ohne daß
a so valuable thing lost go without that

man es wieder erhalte, machte ihn sehr böse. Er
one it again get made him very angry He

hatte auch am Tag vorher das ganze
had also at the day before the whole

Dienstpersonal versammelt, es verhört und
service personal gathered it interrogated and

bedroht und endlich dem Finder eine Belohnung
threatened and finally the finder a reward

ausgesetzt. Das ganze Haus war in Aufruhr über
exposed The whole house was in revolt over

den verlorenen Schmuck.
the lost jewel

Als Moni mit seinen Geißen an der Vorderseite
As Moni with his goats on the front side

des Hauses vorbeiging, stand Paula dort. Sie hatte
of the house passed stood Paula there She had

auf ihn gewartet, es wunderte sie so sehr, ob
on him waited it surprised her so much whether
for

er immer noch nicht wieder singen könne und
he always still not again sing could and

lustig sei. Als er nun vorbeischlich, rief sie: "Moni!
merry be As he now past snuck called she Moni

Moni! Bist du denn auch derselbe Geißbub, der
Moni Are you then also the same goat boy who

vom Morgen bis zum Abend sang:
from the morning until to the evening sang

"'Und so blau ist der Himmel,
And so blue is the sky

Und ich freu mich fast zu Tod'?"
And I rejoice me almost to death

Moni hörte die Worte, er gab keine Antwort, aber
Moni heard the words he gave no answer but

sie machten einen großen Eindruck auf ihn.
they made a large impression on him

Oh, wie war's doch so anders, als er den ganzen
Oh as was it indeed so different as he the whole

Tag singen konnte und er so fröhlich war wie
day sing could and he so merrily was as

seine Lieder. Oh, wenn es doch wieder so sein
his songs Oh when it indeed again so be

könnte!
could

Wieder zog Moni zu seiner Anhöhe hinauf, still
Again pulled Moni to his elevation up quiet

und freudlos und ohne Gesang. Der Regen hatte
and joyless and without singing The rain had

nun aufgehört, aber düster hingen ringsum die
now stopped but bleak hung all around the

Nebel an den Bergen, und der Himmel war noch
fog on the mountains and the sky was still

voll dunkler Wolken. Moni setzte sich wieder
full (of) dark clouds Moni set himself again

unter den Felsen und kämpfte mit seinen
under the rocks and struggled with his

Gedanken. Gegen Mittag fing der Himmel an,
thoughts Against (the) afternoon caught the sky on

sich aufzuklären, es wurde heller und heller.
itself to clear up it became more clear and more clear

Moni kam aus seiner Höhle hervor und schaute
Moni came out of his hollow forth and looked

umher. Die Geißen sprangen wieder lustig hin und
around The goats jumped again merrily here and

her, auch das Zicklein war ganz übermütig
away also the kid was completely over-courageous
cocky

vor Freuden über die wiederkehrende Sonne und
before joy over the returning sun and
of

machte die fröhlichsten Sprünge.
made the most joyful jumps

Moni stand draußen auf der Kanzel und sah, wie
Moni stood outside on the pulpit and saw how

es immer schöner und heller wurde unten
it always more beautiful and more clear became under

im Tal und oben über dem Berge. Jetzt
in the valley and above over the mountains Now

teilten sich die Wolken und der lichtblaue
divided themselves the clouds and the light blue

Himmel schaute so lieblich und freundlich
sky looked so lovely and friendly

herunter. Es war Moni, als schaue der liebe Gott
down It was Moni as look the dear god

aus dem lichten Blau zu ihm nieder. Und auf
from the light blue to him down And at

einmal war es in seinem Herzen ganz klar, was
once was it in his heart completely clear what

er tun mußte, er konnte das Unrecht nicht
he do must he could the wrong not

mehr mit sich herumfragen. Er mußte es
(any)more with himself around ask He must it
           carry around

ablegen. Jetzt ergriff Moni das Zicklein, das neben
lay off Now took Moni the kid that beside
drop off

ihm umhersprang, nahm es in seinen Arm und
him jumped around took it in his arm and

sagte mit Zärtlichkeit: "O Mäggerli, du armes
said with tenderness Oh Mäggerli you poor

Mäggerli! Ich habe gewiß getan, was ich konnte,
Mäggerli I have certainly done what I could

aber es ist ein Unrecht, und das darf man nicht
but it is a wrong and that may one not

tun. Oh, wenn du nur nicht sterben müßtest, ich
do Oh when you only not die must I

kann es nicht aushalten!" Und nun fing Moni so
can it not bear And now caught Moni so
started

sehr zu weinen an, daß er nicht mehr weiter
much to cry -on- that he not (any)more further

reden konnte. Und das Zicklein meckerte wehmütig
talk could And the kid bleated wistfully

und kroch tief unter seinen Arm, als wollte es
and crept deep under his arm as wanted it

sich ganz bei ihm verstecken und in Sicherheit
itself completely at him hide and in security

bringen. Jetzt hob Moni das Geißlein auf seine
bring Now lifted Moni the kid on his

Schultern.
shoulders

"Komm, Mäggerli, ich trage dich noch einmal heim
Come Mäggerli I carry you still once home

heute, vielleicht kann ich dich bald nicht mehr
today perhaps can I you soon not (any)more

tragen."
carry

Als er mit seinen Geißen unten beim Badehaus
As he with his goats under at the bathhouse
hotel

war, wartete Paula schon auf ihn. Moni stellte das
was waited Paula already on him Moni set the
for

Junge mit der Schwarzen in den Stall hinein,
young (one) with the black (one) in the stable inside

und anstatt weiter zu ziehen, wollte er an dem
and instead of further to pull wanted he on the
go

Fräulein vorbei ins Haus gehen. Sie hielt ihn an.
miss past in the house go She held him -on-
stopped

"Immer noch ohne Gesang, Moni?"
Always still without singing Moni

"Ich muß etwas anzeigen", erwiderte Moni.
I must something note answered Moni
tell

"Anzeigen? Was denn? Darf ich's nicht wissen?"
Note What then May I it not know

"Ich muß zum Wirt, es ist etwas gefunden
I must to the host it is something found

worden."
become

"Gefunden? Was denn? Ich habe auch etwas
Found What then I have also something

verloren, ein schönes Kreuz."
lost a beautiful cross

"Ja, das ist es gerade."
Yes that is it just

"Was sagst du?" rief Paula in höchster
What say you called Paula in highest

Überraschung. "Ist es ein Kreuz mit funkelnden
surprise Is it a cross with sparkling

Steinen?"
stones

"Ja."
Yes

"Wo    hast  du's  denn, Moni?  Gib's  doch  her,  hast
Where  have  you it  then    Moni   Give is indeed here  have

du's  gefunden?"
you it     found

"Nein,  der  Jörgli  von  Küblis."
No      the  Jörgli  from  Küblis

Nun  wollte  Paula  wissen,  wer  das  sei,  und   wo   er
Now  wanted  paula  know    who  that  be   and  where  he

wohne,  und  auf  der  Stelle  jemand  nach  Küblis
live    and  on   the  spot    someone  to   Küblis

hinunterschicken,    das    Kreuz  zu  holen.
down under send     (for) the  cross   to   get

"Ich  will  schon  gehen,  und  wenn  er's  noch  hat,
I     want  already  go    and  when  he it  still  has

will  ich's  bringen"  sagte  Moni.
want  I it   bring     said   Moni

"Wenn  er's  noch  hat?"  rief  Paula,  "warum  sollte
When   he it  still  has  called  Paula   why    should

er's nicht mehr haben? Und woher weißt du
he it not (any)more have And from where know you

denn von allem, Moni? Wann hat er's gefunden,
then from all Moni When has he it found
about everything

und wie hast du's denn erfahren?"
and how have you it then experienced
heard

Moni schaute zu Boden. Er durfte nicht sagen,
Moni looked at (the) ground He could not say

wie alles zugegangen war, und wie er geholfen
how everything gone was and as he helped

hatte, den Fund zu verheimlichen, bis er es nicht
had the find to conceal until he it not

mehr hatte ertragen können.
(any)more had endure was able

Aber Paula war sehr gut zu Moni. Sie nahm ihn
But paula was very good to Moni She took him

auf die Seite, setzte sich auf einen Baumstamm
on the side set herself on a tree trunk

zu ihm hin und sagte mit der größten
to him away and said with the greatest
with him

Freundlichkeit: "Komm, erzähl mir alles, wie es
friendliness Come tell me everything how it

gegangen ist, Moni, ich möchte so gern alles
gone is Moni I may so gladly everything

von dir wissen."
from you know

Nun faßte der Moni Zutrauen und fing an und
Now seized the Moni confidence and caught on and
got started

erzählte die ganze Sache. Er berichtete auch, daß
told the whole thing He reported also that

er sich um das Leben von Mäggerli Sorgen
he himself for the life from Mäggerli worry

gemacht habe und wie er so alle Freude verloren
made have and as he so all joy lost

hatte und nicht mehr zum lieben Gott
had and not (any)more to the dear god

aufschauen  durfte.  Heute,  sagte  er,  konnte  er  es
look up          could      Today    said    he    could    he    it

nicht  mehr  länger  ertragen.
not    (any)more  longer    endure

Jetzt  redete  Paula  sehr  freundlich  mit  ihm  und
Now    spoke    Paula    very    friendly      with    him    and

meinte,  er  hätte  nur  gleich  kommen  und
thought    he    had      only    immediately    come      and

alles  anzeigen  sollen.  Und  es  sei  recht,  daß  er
everything    tell        should    And    it    be    right    that    he

ihr  jetzt  alles  so  aufrichtig  gesagt  habe,  er
her    now    everything    so    honestly      told      have    he

solle  es  nicht  bereuen.  Dann  sagte  sie,  dem  Jörgli
should    it    not      regret      Then    said    she    the    Jörgli

könne  er  zehn  Franken  versprechen,  wenn  sie  das
could    he    ten      franks          promise            when    she    the
                          (money)

Kreuz  wieder  in  Händen  habe.
cross    again    in    hands      have

"Zehn Franken?" wiederholte Moni voller
Ten franks repeated Moni with full
(money)

Erstaunen. Denn er wußte ja, daß Jörgli es hatte
astonishment Then he knew yes that Jörgli it had

verkaufen wollen. Jetzt stand Moni auf und sagte,
sell want Now stood Moni up and said

er wollte noch heute nach Küblis hinunter, und
he wanted still today to Küblis down and

wenn er das Kreuz bekäme, es gleich
when he the cross would get it immediately

morgen früh mitbringen. Nun lief er davon
in the morning early bring along Now ran he there-from

und konnte wieder ganz große Sprünge
and could again completely great jumps

machen, er hatte wieder ein viel leichteres Herz,
make he had again a much lighter heart

das schlechte Gewissen belastete ihn nicht mehr.
the bad conscious weighed him not (any)more

Daheim stellte er nur seine Geiß in den Stall,
At home set he only his goat in the stable

sagte der Großmutter, er habe noch einen Auftrag
said the grandmother he have still a mission

auszurichten und rannte gleich nach Küblis
to achieve and ran immediately to Küblis

hinunter. Er fand den Jörgli daheim und sagte ihm,
down He found the Jörgli at home and told him

was er getan hatte. Der war erst sehr
what he done had That one was first very

aufgebracht, aber als er nun erfuhr, daß
brought up but as he now experienced that
upset heard

alles bekannt sei, zog er das Kreuz heraus
everything known be pulled he the cross out

und fragte: "Gibt sie mir auch etwas dafür?"
and asked Gives she me also something therefore

"Ja, jetzt kannst du sehen, Jörgli", sagte Moni
Yes now can you see Jörgli said Moni

entrüstet, "auf dem ehrlichen Weg hättest du
indignant on the honest way had you

gleich zehn Franken bekommen und auf deinem
immediately ten franks become and on your
(money)

Lügenweg doch nur vier."
lie way indeed only four

Jörgli war sehr überrascht. Jetzt reute es ihn,
Jörgli was very surprised Now regretted it him

daß er nicht gleich mit dem Kreuz ins
that he not immediately with the cross in the

Badehaus gegangen war, nachdem er es vor der
bathhouse gone was after he it before the
hotel

Tür aufgelesen hatte. Denn er hatte doch nun
door picked up had Then he had indeed now

kein gutes Gewissen und hätte
no good conscious and had

es anders haben können. Aber jetzt war's zu spät.
it different have been able But now was it too late
been able to have it differently

Er    übergab    das    Kreuz    dem    Moni,    und    dieser
He    handed over    the    cross    to the    Moni    and    this one

eilte    damit    heim,  es  war  draußen  schon  dunkel
hurried    there-with    home  it  was  outside  already  dark

geworden.
become

# Moni singt wieder
## *Moni Sings Again*

Paula hatte angeordnet, daß man sie am frühen
Paula had ordered that one her at the early

Morgen wecken sollte. Wenn der Geißbub
morning wake should When the goat boy

käme, wollte sie selbst mit ihm verhandeln.
would come wanted she herself with him deal

Am Abend hatte sie noch eine lange Unterredung
At the evening had she still a long conversation

mit dem Wirt gehabt und war dann sehr befriedigt
with the host had and was then very satisfied

aus seiner Stube herausgekommen. Sie mußte
out of his room come out She must

etwas Erfreuliches mit ihm ausgemacht haben.
something joyful with him made out have
decided

Als der Geißbub am Morgen mit seiner Herde
As the goat boy at the morning with his herd

herankam, stand Paula schon vor dem Haus und
came up stood Paula already in front the house and

rief: "Moni, kannst du denn immer noch nicht
called Moni can you then ever still not

singen?"
sing

Er schüttelte den Kopf: "Nein, ich kann's nicht, ich
He shook the head No I can not I

muß jetzt immer an das Mäggerli denken, wie
must now always on the Mäggerli think as

lange es noch mit mir geht. Ich kann nicht mehr
long it still with me goes I can no more

singen, solange ich lebe, und hier ist das Kreuz."
sing as long as I live and here is the cross

Damit übergab er ein kleines Päckchen, denn
So handed over he a little package because

die Großmutter hatte es ihm sorgfältig in drei
the grandmother had it (for) him carefully in three

oder vier Papiere gewickelt.
or four papers wrapped

Paula schälte das Kreuz aus den Hüllen heraus
Paula peeled the cross out the envelop out

und betrachtete es genau. Es war wirklich ihr
and regarded it exactly It was really her

schönes Kreuz mit den funkelnden Steinen und
beautiful cross with the sparkling stones and

völlig unversehrt.
totally intact

"So, Moni", sagte sie nun freundlich, "du hast mir
Sp Moni said she now friendly you have me

eine große Freude gemacht, denn ohne dich
one great happiness made then without you

hätte ich wohl mein Kreuz nie mehr gesehen.
would have I well my cross never more seen

Nun will ich dir auch eine Freude machen. Geh,
Now will I you also a happiness make Go

hol das Mäggerli dort aus dem Stall, es gehört
get the Mäggerli there out the stable it belongs

jetzt dir!"
now to you

Moni starrte das Fräulein mit einem Erstaunen an,
Moni stared the miss with an astonishment on

als sei es unmöglich, ihre Worte zu verstehen.
as be it impossible her words to understand

Endlich stotterte er: "Aber wie — wie könnte das
Finally stuttered he But how how could the

Mäggerli mein sein?"
Mäggerli mine be

"Wie?" wiederholte Paula lächelnd, "sieh, gestern
How repeated Paula smiling see yesterday

abend hab ich es dem Wirt abgekauft und heute
evening have I it the host bought of and today

morgen schenke ich es dir. Kannst du jetzt wieder
morning give I it you Can you now again

singen?"
sing

"Oh!" stieß Moni hervor und rannte wie ein
Oh uttered Moni forth and ran as a

Unsinniger auf den Stall zu, zog das Geißlein
madman on the stable towards pulled the kid

heraus und nahm es auf den Arm. Dann kam er
out and took it on the arm Then came he

zurückgesprungen und streckte dem Fräulein seine
jumped back and extended the miss his

Hand entgegen und sagte immer wieder: "Ich
hand towards and said always again I

danke tausendmal! Vergelt's Gott! Und wenn ich
thank (a) thousand time(s) Makes up it god And when I

Ihnen nur einen Gefallen tun könnte!"
you only a pleasure do could

"Dann sing mir dein Lied", sagte Paula.
Then sing me your song said Paula

Da stimmte Moni sein Lied an und zog nun
There tuned Moni his song on and pulled now
started moved

den Berg hinauf mit den Geißen, und seine
the mountain up with the goats and his

Jubeltöne schmetterten so ins Tal hinab, daß
cheerful tunes threw so in the valley down that

im ganzen Badehaus keiner war, der sie nicht
in the whole bathhouse none was who them not
hotel

hörte. Und mancher drehte sich auf seinem
heard And many turned themselves on their

Kissen um und sagte: "Der Geißbub hat wieder
pillow around and said The goat boy has again

gute Laune." Es freute aber alle, daß er wieder
good mood It pleased however all that he again

sang, denn sie hatten sich alle an den
sang then they had themselves all on the

| | | | | | |
|---|---|---|---|---|---|
| fröhlichen | Wecker | gewöhnt, | die | einen | zum |
| joyful | waker<br>alarm | used | which | one | at the |

| | | | | |
|---|---|---|---|---|
| Aufstehen, | die | anderen | zum | Weiterschlafen. Als |
| stand up<br>awakening | the | others | to the | further sleep(ing) As |

| | | | | | | | |
|---|---|---|---|---|---|---|---|
| Moni | oben | von | der | ersten | Höhe | das | Fräulein |
| Moni | above | from | the | first | height | the | miss |

| | | | | | | | |
|---|---|---|---|---|---|---|---|
| immer | noch | unten | vor | dem | Haus | stehen | sah, |
| always | still | under | before | the | house | stand | saw |

| | | | | | | | |
|---|---|---|---|---|---|---|---|
| trat | er | extra | weit | hinaus | und | sang | hinunter, so |
| stepped | he | extra | far | out | and | sang | down so<br>as |

| | | |
|---|---|---|
| laut | er | konnte: |
| loud | he<br>as he | could |

| | | | | | |
|---|---|---|---|---|---|
| "Und | so | blau | ist | der | Himmel, |
| And | so | blue | is | the | sky |

| | | | | | | |
|---|---|---|---|---|---|---|
| Und | ich | freu | mich | fast | zu | Tod!" |
| And | I | rejoice | myself | almost | to | death |

| | | | | | | | | |
|---|---|---|---|---|---|---|---|---|
| Den | ganzen | Tag | über | sang | der | Moni | und | alle |
| The | whole | day | over | sang | the | Moni | and | all |

Geißen wurden angesteckt von seiner Fröhlichkeit
goats became on-stuck from his happiness
infected

und hüpften und sprangen umher. Es war, als
and hopped and jumped around It was as

ob ein großes Fest gefeiert würde. Die Sonne
whether a large firmly celebrated would The sun

schien fröhlich vom blauen Himmel herunter.
shone merrily from the blue sky down

Und nach dem großen Regen waren auch alle
And after the great rain were also all

Kräutlein frisch und die gelben und roten
little herbs fresh and the yellow and red

Blümlein glänzten. Moni glaubte, Berg und Tal
little flowers shone Moni believed mountain and valley

und die ganze Welt noch nie so schön gesehen
and the whole world still never so beautiful seen

zu haben. Sein Zicklein ließ er den ganzen Tag
to have His kid let he the whole day

nicht aus den Augen. Er zog ihm die besten
not from the eyes He pulled it the best

Kräutlein aus und fütterte es und sagte immer
little herbs out and fed it and said always

wieder: "Mäggerli, du gutes Mäggerli, du
again Mäggerli you good Mäggerli you

mußt nicht sterben, du bist jetzt mein und
must not die you are now mine and
don't have to

kommst mit mir auf die Weide hinauf, solange
come with me on the meadow up as long (as)

wir leben." Und mit schallendem Singen und Jodeln
we live And with resounding singing and yodeling

kam Moni auch am Abend wieder hinunter.
came Moni also at the evening again down

Nachdem er die Schwarze zu ihrem Stall geführt
After he the black (one) to her stable led

hatte, nahm er das Zicklein auf den Arm, es kam
had took he the kid on the arm it came

ja nun mit ihm nach Haus. Das Mäggerli
yes now with him to (the) house The Mäggerli
indeed

machte auch gar keine Anstalten, als wollte es
made also at all no moves as wanted it

lieber dableiben, sondern schmiegte sich an den
rather there-stay but snuggled itself on the

Moni. Bei ihm fühlte es sich geborgen, denn Moni
Moni With him felt it itself secure since Moni

hatte es ja schon lange besser und zärtlicher
had it yes already long better and more tender

behandelt als die eigene Mutter.
treated as the own mother

Als aber Moni zu der Großmutter kam, sein
As however Moni to the grandmother came his

Mäggerli auf der Schulter, da wußte diese gar
Mäggerli on the shoulder there knew this one at all

nicht, was geschehen war. Denn Monis Rufen: "Es
not what happened was Then Moni's call It
had

gehört mir, Großmutter, es gehört mir!" erklärte
belongs me grandmother it belongs me explained

ihr die Sache noch lange nicht. Aber Moni konnte
her the thing still long not But moni could

noch nicht erzählen. Erst lief er zu dem Stall und
still not tell First ran he to the stable and

dort, hart neben der Braunen, damit es sich
there right next to the brown (one) there-with it itself
so

nicht fürchte, machte er dem Mäggerli ein
not fear (would) made he the Mäggerli a

schönes, weiches Lager aus frischem Stroh. Er
beautiful soft bed from fresh straw He

legte es darauf und sagte: "So Mäggerli, nun
put it thereupon and said So Mäggerli now

schlaf gut in der neuen Heimat. So sollst du's
sleep well in the new home So will you it

immer haben, alle Tage mache ich dir ein neues
always have all days make I you a new

Bettlein."
little bed

| Erst | jetzt | kam | Moni | zu | der | verwunderten |
|------|-------|-----|------|-----|-----|--------------|
| First | now | came | Moni | to | the | surprised |

| Großmutter | zurück, | und | wie | sie | nun | zusammen |
|------------|---------|-----|-----|-----|-----|----------|
| grandmother | back | and | as | they | now | together |

| bei | ihrem | Abendessen | saßen, | erzählte | er | ihr | die |
|-----|-------|------------|--------|----------|-----|-----|-----|
| at | her | evening dinner | sat | told | he | her | the |

| ganze | Geschichte | von | Anfang | an. | Er |
|-------|------------|-----|--------|-----|-----|
| whole | story | from | (the) beginning | -on- | He |

| berichtete | von | seinen | drei | kummervollen | Tagen |
|------------|-----|--------|------|--------------|-------|
| reported | from | his | three | sorrowful | days |

| und | dem | heutigen | beglückenden | Schluß. | Die |
|-----|-----|----------|--------------|---------|-----|
| and | the | today | exhilerating | end | The |

| Großmutter | hörte | ganz | still | und | aufmerksam |
|------------|-------|------|-------|-----|------------|
| grandmother | heard | completely | quiet | and | attentive |

| zu, | und | als | er | zu | Ende | war, | sagte | sie | ernsthaft: |
|-----|-----|-----|-----|-----|------|------|-------|-----|------------|
| to | and | as | he | at | (the) end | was | said | she | seriously |

"Moni, wie es dir jetzt gegangen ist, daran sollst
Moni  how  it  you  now  gone  is  there-on  will

du immer denken. Während du dir Sorgen um
you always think While you yourself worries for

das Geißlein machtest, hatte der liebe Gott ihm
the kid made had the dear god him

schon lange geholfen und dir zur Freude einen
already long helped and you to the joy a

Weg gefunden. Er hat dir geholfen, weil du dein
way found He has you helped because you your

Unrecht eingesehen hast. Hättest du sofort
wrong in-seen have Had you immediately

recht getan und auf Gott vertraut, so wäre
right done and on god trusted so would be

gleich alles gut gegangen. Jetzt hat der
immediately everything good gone Now has the

liebe Gott dir so sehr geholfen, daß du es dein
dear god you so very helped that you it your

Leben lang nicht vergessen darfst."
life · long · not · forget · may

"Nein, ich will es auch nie vergessen", sagte Moni
No · I · want · it · also · never · forget · said · Moni

mit eifriger Zustimmung, "und gewiß immer
with · zealous · approval · and · certainly · always

gleich denken: Ich muß nur tun, was vor dem
immediately · think · I · must · only · do · what · before · the

lieben Gott recht ist, das andere bringt er
dear · god · right · is · the · other (things) · brings · he

schon in Ordnung."
already · in · order

Bevor aber Moni sich schlafen legen konnte,
Before · however · Moni · himself · sleep · lay · could

mußte er noch einmal in den Stall und sein
must · he · still · once · in · the · stable · and · his

Geißlein anschauen, ob es auch wirklich
kid · look at · whether · it · also · really

möglich sei, daß es draußen liege und ihm gehöre.
possible be that it outside lie and him belong

Der Jörgli bekam seine zehn Franken, aber so
The Jörgli got his ten franks but so
(money)

leicht sollte er denn doch nicht von der Sache
easily should he then indeed not from the thing

loskommen.
loose come

Als er wieder ins Badehaus kam, wurde er vor
As he again in the bathhouse came became he before
hotel

den Wirt geführt. Er nahm den Buben beim
the host led He took the boy at the

Kragen, schüttelte ihn tüchtig und sagte
collar shook him thoroughly and said

bedrohlich: "Jörgli! Jörgli! Versuch du kein
threateningly Jörgli Jörgli Try you no

zweitesmal mehr, mein ganzes Haus in Mißkredit
second time (any)more my whole house in discredit

zu bringen! Kommt noch ein einziges Mal
to bring Comes still a single time
        Happens

so etwas vor, so kommst du auf eine Art aus
so something before so come you on a way from
something like this

meinem Haus hinaus, die dir nicht gefällt! Sieh,
my house out which you not pleases Look

dort oben steckt ein ganz kräftiges
there above sticks a completely powerful

Weidenrütchen für solche Fälle. Jetzt geh und denk
willow rusk for such cases Now go and think

dran!"
there-on

Aber noch eine Folge hatte der Vorgang für
But still one consequence had the process for

den Buben: Wenn von nun an irgend etwas im
the boy When from now on any something in the

Badehaus verloren gegangen war, rief die ganze
bathhouse lost gone was called the whole
hotel

Dienerschaft sofort: "Das hat der Jörgli von
*servantship immediately That has the Jörgli from*

Küblis!" Und kam dieser nachher ins Haus, so
*Küblis And came this one after in the house so*

drangen sie alle miteinander auf ihn ein und
*pressed they all with each other on him in and*

riefen: "Gib's her, Jörgli! Gib's heraus!" Und wie
*called Give it here Jörgli Give it out And as*

sehr er auch versicherte, er habe nichts und wisse
*much he also assured he have nothing and knew*

nichts, sie schrien ihn alle an: "Dich kennt man
*nothing they screamed him all to You knows one*

schon! Uns betrügst du nicht!"
*already Us deceive you not*

So hatte der Jörgli immer die bedrohlichsten
*So had the Jörgli always the most threatening*

Angriffe zu bestehen und hatte fast keinen
*attacks to exist and had almost no*
         *suffer*

ruhigen Augenblick mehr. Denn wenn er jetzt
calm moment (any)more Then when he now

nur jemand auf sich zukommen sah, so glaubte
only someone on himself to come saw so believed

er schon, der komme, um ihn zu fragen: "Hast
he already that one come for him to ask Have

du nicht dies oder das gefunden?" So war es dem
you not this or that found So was it the

Jörgli nie mehr recht wohl zumut, und
Jörgli never (any)more right well at the mood and

hundertmal dachte er: "Hätte ich doch jenes
(a) hundred times thought he Had I indeed that

Kreuz auf der Stelle zurückgegeben, in meinem
cross on the spot given back in my

ganzen Leben behalte ich nichts mehr, das mir
whole life keep I nothing (any)more that me

nicht gehört."
not belongs

Der   Moni   aber         hörte         den   ganzen
The   Moni   however      heard         the   whole
                          (hörte auf; stopped)

Sommer  nicht  auf  zu  singen  und  zu  jodeln,  denn
summer   not    up   to   sing    and  to  yodel   since

er   fühlte   sich   so   wohl   da   oben   bei   seinen
he   felt   himself  so   well   there  up   with   his

Geißen,   wie   kaum   ein   anderer   Mensch   auf   der
goats      as   hardly   an   other    human    on    the

Welt. Aber   oft,   wenn   er   so   in   seiner   Zufriedenheit
world  But   often   when   he   so   in   his     satisfaction

ausgestreckt   auf   der   Felsenkanzel   lag   und   in   das
stretched out   on   the   rock-pulpit    lay   and   in   the

sonnige   Tal   hinabschaute,   mußte   er   daran
sunny    valley   looked down    must    he   there-on

denken,   wie   er   damals   mit   seinem   schlechten
think     how   he   at that time  with   his    bad

Gewissen   unter   dem   Regenfelsen   saß.   Und   er   sagte
conscious   under   the   rain-rock     sat   And   he   said

jedesmal laut vor sich hin: "Ich weiß schon, wie
each time loud before himself away I know already how

ich's mache, daß es nie mehr so kommt. Ich
I it do that it never (any)more so comes I

tue nichts mehr, wenn ich dabei nicht fröhlich
do nothing (any)more when I there-by not happy

in den Himmel aufsehen kann, weil es dem
in the sky see up can because it the

lieben Gott so recht ist."
dear god so right is

Geschah es aber, daß der Moni sich zu lange
Happened it however that the Moni himself too long

in seine Betrachtungen vertiefte, so kam die eine
in his observations immersed so came the one

oder die andere der Geißen heran. Sie schaute
or the other of the goats near They looked

verwundert nach ihm aus und versuchte ihn zur
surprised after him out and tried him to the

Gesellschaft zurückzumeckern, was er aber
company back to bleat what he however

manchmal ziemlich lange nicht hörte. Nur wenn
sometimes rather long not heard Only when

sein Mäggerli kam und mit Verlangen nach ihm
his Mäggerli came and with desire to him

rief, dann hörte er es gleich. Er lief ihm auch
called then heard he it immediately He ran him also

sofort entgegen, denn es sein anhängliches
immediately towards since it his affectionate

Geißlein war und es blieb Monis liebstes Gut.
kid was and it remained Moni's dearest good